Some Time with
Eagles
and
Falcons

Jerry Olsen

hancock

house

ISBN 0-88839-375-X
Copyright © 1995 Jerry Olsen

Cataloging in Publication Data
Olsen, Jerry
    Some time with eagles and falcons

    ISBN 0-88839-375-X

    1. Olsen, Jerry   2. Eagles.   3. Falcons.   I. Title.
QL696.F3047 1995   598.9'1   C95-910319-8

Published simultaneously in Canada and the United States by

HANCOCK HOUSE PUBLISHERS LTD.
19313 Zero Avenue, Surrey, B.C. V4P 1M7
(604) 538-1114   Fax (604) 538-2262

HANCOCK HOUSE PUBLISHERS
1431 Harrison Avenue, Blaine, WA 98230-5005
(604) 538-1114   Fax (604) 538-2262

for Peter and Anna

Cover design by Alan Nicol, Anna Olsen
and Alan Vogt

Illustrations by Robert Bartos

CONTENTS

		Page
Preface / Acknowledgements		vii
1.	A Beginning and an End	1
2.	Roslyn and Trapping Falcons	9
3.	Pullman	15
4.	Nesting Around Port Augusta	25
5.	Hunting Around Port Augusta	35
6.	Sydney Airport and Port Lincoln	45
7.	Rehabilitation and Filming	55
8.	At the Movies	85
9.	The Solomon Islands	93
10.	Canberra Falcons & Eagles	105
11.	Back in the U.S.A.	119
12.	Refuge	131
Appendix 1-Handbook for Rehabilitating Orphaned and Injured Raptors		137

PREFACE and ACKNOWLEDGEMENTS

The purpose of this book is to tell a story about some of the people, hawks, eagles and falcons I knew over the past twenty-five years. Conservation and rehabilitation of raptors has grown from what it was then. Hopefully, some will find interest in a story about ties between people and raptors in a different time.

I am particularly grateful to Sue Trost who spent many hours working on this book. Thanks also to a number of other generous friends who read parts or all of the book in its early stages. These include Stephen Debus, Peter Meredith, Greg Hayes, Nick Mooney and Ian Warden. A number of people offered invaluable assistance in the field including Terry Billet, Don Fletcher, Neil Reckord, Jeanine Randall, Debbie Worner, Wally Truesdale, Libby Stephenson, Frank Barnes, Tanya May, Stephen Turner, David Mallinson, Terry and Helen Dennis, Peter and Pat Slater, Robert Bartos, Sue Trost, Brian Terrill, Dave Borman, Brett McNamara, Rob Watchorn, Richard Phelps, Steve Welch, Julie Crawford, Virginia Logan, Tony Brownlie, Paul Higginbotham, Peter Hann, and Teu Zingihite. For helpful discussions about rehabilitation, and about raptors, I thank Tom Aumann, Nick Mooney, Stephen Debus, David Baker-Gabb, Steve Wilson, Bruce Haak, Tom Cade, Ian Newton, Derek Ratcliffe, Katie Jodrell, Phil Paine and Bill Burnham. I am grateful to Pat and Terry Goss for allowing me to lock myself in their upstairs in Perth for a week to work on this book and to my sisters, Debra Stone and Deana Withey who taught me so much about caring for animals, though they may not have realized it at the time. Thanks to Noel Vanzetti, Warren Atkins and John Dowden for excellent, professional help with computer processing. My particular thanks to Greg Hayes who helped to set up the current raptor research in the A.C.T.

1 A Beginning and an End

Lake Lebarge in the early morning light can be a sacred place but sometimes it can be a place to fear. The fog that rests on the water some mornings in the Yukon summer is unearthly and delicate and the sun can be a glowing red ball among misted fir trees. Only two other people lived on the great lake besides John Lago and me. The two fishermen, named Jake and George, argued a lot, particularly after they drank whisky, and neither had visited John's cabin for over three weeks. For some reason they had disappeared. So John first travelled to Richthoffen Island in the middle of the lake to check the spot where the men normally buried their fish on the white sandy beach. They preserved it there under the sand before transporting it by water, and then by road, to Whitehorse some 30 miles south. The fish were there in the sand and starting to smell. Clearly the fishermen were in some trouble or had decided to travel off Lake Lebarge without telling John. So we paddled out to look for them in a small fibreglass canoe. Sometimes we used a little one-horse motor but mostly we paddled along the 70 mile shore of Lebarge, sleeping on the beach when we tired and generally ignored the time of day or night. It was still quite light at one or two A.M.

After two days searching we pushed the canoe through the dead-quiet mist in a reedy swamp on the west end of the lake. A form lying on the shore looked like their boat. At the time I felt unsettled and feared that we might find a body or two bodies under the boat. The mist deadened any sound in the swamp except the oars dipping and the prow cutting through the lake and I was breathing louder than before.

The boat was upturned so John looked under it while I searched along the shore for any sign of Jake and George. But we found no bodies there. Inside the boat we could see how they tied their pots, pans and some fishing gear to the seats. The gear was twisted and tangled as if the boat had rolled over many times before the reeds on the west side of the lake arrested it.

John and I said nothing to each other during the last hour of paddling. My mouth was dry and I stayed quiet but John suddenly remarked "I wonder if they killed each other. I bet they had one of their fights and Jake killed George or George killed Jake and whoever was left went into the bush to hide from the Mounties". My explanation was less imaginative- "Perhaps. But storms come down from nowhere on Lebarge and we've been caught before. If a storm hit and the boat rolled over, they wouldn't last 10 minutes in this water. I think they're in the lake."

As we talked on about the dead men, because we believed that probably they had died, I started to drift back, remembering bodies I'd seen before. Both times it was on the Colville Indian Reservation near Spokane in Washington State. Once a man was killed by a horse in front of us during a rodeo at Inchelium. The horse's hooves went straight through the Indian's back. My father was a doctor and tried to save the rodeo rider by giving him mouth to mouth in the ambulance all the way to Colville, an hour away. The man was dirty and drunk when he got onto the bucking horse and my father told us afterwards how angry he was that he'd worked so hard to save him while a doctor in Colville said he shouldn't have bothered. My father couldn't bring him back to life in the ambulance. Whatever the man's dreams, his ties to others living stopped there under the horse's hooves.

Another time a plane crashed in view of the road, nose-dived into the ground. We rushed over to the plane, and the man inside, smelling of beer, was smashed against the dash and wheel. There were about ten people standing around the downed plane when we pulled him out. The man was moving, inhaling, and groaning but my father looked into his eyes and told us there was no hope, no hope in his eyes. He moved and made noise but he was gone. Under the first man we found another, both probably about forty, and he did as the first and he too was gone. They had landed in a field near Inchelium to get some beer and tried to take off again, their last act before crashing the plane nose-first into the field.

Those of us who work with raptors know about mortality. This is the essence of falcons and eagles; they kill other animals. Even with this daily exposure to killing, the nature of falcons and eagles, we still find it hard to see our own species, or a species we identify with, dead before us. We never grow accustomed to it or feel easy about it, and we shouldn't. By placing ourselves inside the mind and life of an animal, we know what they've lost. We value that life. Our drive to conserve and rehabilitate species rests on this conviction.

A man named Robert Service once wrote a poem called **The Cremation of Sam Mcgee** about a corpse on Lake Lebarge during the gold rush when steamers used to paddle up the Yukon River into the lake-

    "There are strange things done in the midnight sun
    by the men who moil for gold
    The Arctic trails have their secret tales that would
    make your blood run cold.
    The Northern lights have seen queer sites but the
    queerest I ever did see.
    Was the night on the marge of Lake Lebarge where
    I cremated Sam McGee ..."

The poem ran through my head that morning as we searched the reeds and shoreline for Jake and George. A Belted Kingfisher suddenly flew along the forest edge chasing a North-

ern Goshawk who cackled with indignity and tried to turn
on the kingfisher and snare it. Finally the kingfisher drove
the goshawk away. We looked for another hour and, as we
moved off the shore into the dark conifer woods, Red Squirrels chattered warnings to each other and marked our pro-
gression through the forest. But we found nothing more and
decided to leave for the eastern shore and find some way
down to Whitehorse so we could tell the Mounties what we
had and had not found. The mystery needed professional
attention from people who had the time and desire to look
for bodies, or at least they were paid to try. John and I wanted
to explore the clean wild forests and mountains in this part
of the Yukon and not be hampered by responsibility. So we
paddled and drove into Whitehorse, informed the Mounties
and led Constable Andy Anderson to the place in the swamp
where we'd found the boat. The Mounties started an inves-
tigation that day so we were free.

Earlier that spring of 1969 I'd left Spokane to work my way
north on a fishing trawler and then get a job in an Alaskan
sawmill. On a weekend trip from Haines to Whitehorse I
found John and his Volkswagen van with a broken piston
on an isolated, dusty section of the road. We towed the car
into Whitehorse with my old Chevrolet bought for $25 in
Haines. Soon after that I had a fairly serious accident at
work and went to John's cabin to live. Much of our food
came from flour and rice but we netted fish in the lake or
caught Arctic Grayling with home-made flies built from fishing hooks, feathers gathered from the beach and twigs. Often we smoked this fish by lighting the wood stove with
pieces of alder and extending the chimney pipes several
yards out so the smoke was cold and the fish didn't cook.
Cheese and eggs lasted four or five weeks in the "fridge"
John had built beneath the floorboards of the cabin but they
tended to go off slightly and affect our behaviour if we ate
them later than that. That's what we thought anyway. We
read a lot in our spare time including Steinbeck and William
James, particularly "Varieties of Religious Experience" so
appropriate to the life we led on the lake. The forest around
Lebarge is an open park of deciduous and conifer trees. It
was easy to walk there and we took long hikes over many

days. Grizzly Bears were fairly common on Lebarge but mostly they stayed away from us. We carried a .44 magnum pistol for protection, even though pistols were illegal in Canada. But the locals told us that the best protection from a charging bear, or man, was a shotgun blast to the face that could shoot out the eyes or other senses. Realising the logic of this argument we also carried a shotgun.

John grew up in Oshkosh Wisconsin and began work in a factory there. He hated the work and dreamed of travelling to the Yukon to build a cabin at a place he found a year earlier. After breaking his arm in the factory, John used his convalescence to travel to the Yukon to live. He built a superb log cabin while he still had a broken arm and this cabin protected him from summer and winter weather in the Yukon where temperatures sometimes dropped to 60 degrees below zero.

John affected people, he left his mark on them. At 26 years old he showed a reverence for the Yukon, the animals and the people there, that put him above most of us who still weren't sure about our priorities. His height, quiet manner and great skills in building and living in the woods were a common topic of conversation in Whitehorse bars. People were in awe of him, particularly the Indians who were never alone and couldn't understand how John lived on Lake Lebarge alone through winter and summer. He tried to teach us, even those 20 years older than him, about self reliance and how to immerse ourselves in the forest so we could feel empathy and brotherhood with the wilderness. Because he felt these things from inside the web that tied things together, he would sometimes disapprove if we shot a grouse or snowshoe hare to eat. It took some time for us to realise why he was right.

He told us of one of the boldest, most loyal acts he saw on Lebarge. A Sharp-shinned Hawk caught a Grey Jay and held it on the ground trying to kill it. Another Grey Jay came in and risked its life trying to get under the hawk and push it off. The jay eventually succeeded and both jays escaped. This wasn't a story about hawks as bad and jays as

5

good because John greatly admired the wolves, hawks and other predators on the lake and he knew they had to eat. No, this was an allegory about bravery, loyalty and selflessness. These were some of the things he tried to teach us at the time.

The Yukon had a lot of outlaws in those days, men who didn't fit. They came from down south, some needed to hide from the law and some just hated people. If they went only by their first name, nobody asked about their last name, their background or why they came alone to the Yukon. In summer the men lived in tents in camps but most went south for the winter. Jake and George were such men but one, 'Wigwam Harry', astounded the townspeople by living through the Yukon winter in a cardboard box. These men generally got on well with the local Athabaskan Indians though each group tended to stay with their own and the Indians could be suspicious and wary of whites. It could work both ways and distrust grew that summer when Indian kids started a business stealing local dogs and selling them to the tourists. They stole the dog that John and I kept for the fishermen and we tried to find it in Whitehorse and nearby Indian camps. There was some sense of responsibility to Jake and George who may or may not return for their dog. Jake had gone to sleep at John's cabin one afternoon after drinking a lot of whisky and he woke up yelling that something was going to go wrong. He was white with fear and asked John to keep the dog in case something did happen. I prefer to see Jake's ravings and his claims of imminent doom as coincidence because things like that often happened in the North. But John always saw Jake's dream as a premonition.

A week after we found the upturned boat in the swamp, John decided to celebrate my 21st birthday in the isolated cabin on the east side of Lebarge. In the ceremony he included a thick candle stuck in the top of a cornbread cake, smoked ling-cod and Arctic Grayling, wild strawberries, cheese and some whisky. Three days after that, on the 20th of July 1969, we noticed two immature Bald Eagles down the shore from the cabin eating something on the beach.

We had been searching Lebarge looking for falcons, Per-egrines or Merlins, but we commonly saw Bald Eagles, Golden Eagles and Goshawks along the shore and looked for their nests to determine what they preyed on. I left John at the cabin and walked half a mile down the shore and flushed the eagles. Surprisingly, nothing at all appeared on the spot where the eagles had been feeding, or so it seemed, so I looked more closely in the water and along the shore to find any remnants of their prey. Suddenly I saw a hand waving in the water, attached to an arm and a body and realized I had been standing over a dead man lying face down mostly submerged in the water. He had only a small tassel of hair left on the crown of his head and he smelled sulfurous, the rotten eggs smell of ammonium. I guess I hadn't seen him, even though his right leg lay at my feet, because we see what we expect and I hadn't expected or wanted to find a body. The eagles couldn't get through the boot covering his foot that stuck out onto the beach so they had torn open his pants leg and these U.S. national em-blems had been eating the dead man's calf. I thought this must be one of our fishermen but didn't want to stay there alone with a body so I walked back to the cabin to tell John what lay on our shore. In truth, I probably ran. He walked down to the place with me and, while I turned the body over, John looked into the man's face. It was neither of the missing fishermen, it was someone else.

The only thing to do was try to canoe back across the lake, get to Whitehorse and find Andy Anderson to explain what we found. But Lake Lebarge turned very dangerous over the next three days and the high winds and storms kept us at the cabin with the body down the shore. Several times I woke up sweating from bad dreams that the corpse, cov-ered in weeds, pounded on our door and demanded to come in and receive shelter from the Yukon storm. I have trouble now, older and living in the city, identifying with the way we felt then. The isolation and sacred strangeness of Lebarge meant we saw the world differently and we started to be-lieve and feel as our Indian friends believed and felt. This event must have meaning, we must revere as well as fear this man and we could be in danger if we didn't conduct ourselves as we should. So for three days John, the corpse and I waited out the storm over Lebarge. At the end of the third day we saw a small break in the weather and, though it was risky, decided to take the chance of facing a new blow-up of the storm while we crossed the lake. We escaped to the west shore. The crossing frightened us and the storm did blow up as we reached the middle of the lake, but all fears are relative and we were driven to cross anyway.

We expected some trouble when we entered the Mounties' office though the officers were busy talking about NASA landing the first man on the moon and didn't want to talk business. When we told them why we came into Whitehorse they looked askance at each other and at us and asked why we attracted this sort of luck. We answered a number of hard questions then they organised a float plane to fly out with a body bag and collect what the eagles had left. It turned out that the man, Owen Charlie, a local Indian, lived in Whitehorse and police had charged him with manslaughter after he killed his sister. Owen stayed in the Yukon Prison for some years but, when he came out, faced Indian law. He was killed, thrown off the bridge at Whitehorse, and floated down the river to Lake Lebarge where, the Mounties said, he had probably been underwater in the cold lake for a month then surfaced near our cabin.

We found no falcons on Lake Lebarge and no-one ever found the fishermen or Owen Charlie's murderer. To us the Yukon was paradise where we could learn about self reliance, wilderness and mortality. Soon after, I decided to travel south through Washington state but John decided to stay on Lebarge. We'd learned different things from Owen Charlie.

2 Roslyn and Trapping Falcons on the Plains

Roslyn sits on the eastern flanks of the Cascade mountains, the dry side of those mountains, in Washington State. It still looks like a frontier town with the same board houses and store fronts as it did back in 1969 and 1970 when I lived there. Apparently television writers chose Roslyn to be 'Cicely, Alaska' in 'Northern Exposure' because of this frontier look. The town did look Alaskan but the country-side and open fir and Ponderosa Pine forest give it away. Those trees don't grow in Alaska.

Researchers now study Spotted Owls near Roslyn and Cle Elum because populations of these owls still live and breed in the local mountains. A fair number of loggers also live there so the fight over who owns the forest is particularly bitter. Something about the fight is reported almost every day in the local or national news. Loggers and conservationists take each other to court and owl researchers have even been told they have to legally defend, in court, all their scientific findings about the owl. Loggers use the Spotted Owl to show what's wrong with the conservation movement, the conservation movement uses the Spotted Owl to show what's wrong with government policy on logging. The owl has united and sharply focussed both groups.

9

Back in 1969 the loggers cut the forest with few restrictions and the Spotted Owl was an obscure or unknown species to most of us. The conflict was decades ahead. At the time I worked for a Canadian company that explored for minerals and laid mining claims on U.S. land in the Cascade Mountains. This could be harsh work, particularly when we used pack animals to reach isolated sections of the mountains and camped out overnight in the winter snow. On weekends we could look for, and trap Kestrels, Prairie Falcons, Merlins and Gyrfalcons on the farms and sagebrush plains to the east of Roslyn. This obsession used all our time and money.

With Alan Gardner, from Spokane, I made about a dozen trips that winter. Each weekend we cannibalised two old Chevrolets, a 1952 and a 1953, to ensure the trips always happened. When possible, we kept both cars fixed but, when one or both broke down, we took the generator, tires or carburettor or whatever was needed from one to keep the other going.

Falcons set up winter territories and vigorously defend them on the snow-covered plains. In winter the fitness of each raptor is severely tested and these tests were evident to us as we searched. Prairie Falcons nest in the local cliff and gorge country but come up onto the plains in winter to hunt small birds, especially Horned Larks. They defend their territorial boundaries with force. These falcons often chased other falcons, eagles and hawks cacking and screaming in rage until the intruder submitted and flew off. The females in particular showed no fear of any bird even though they were smaller than most raptor species in the area. Force and bluff succeeded on the winter plains.

We drove miles of highway and back roads until we saw the upright form on a telephone pole or crossarm that could be a raptor. With experience we identified each species as soon as we got the binoculars on it. But we couldn't do this at first. A large upright form on a pole could be a Raven, Red-tailed Hawk, Golden Eagle, Prairie Falcon, Rough-legged Hawk or even a Gyrfalcon, the rarest falcon species on the

Washington plains and the one we most wanted to trap. Rough-legged Hawks are a large white or, sometimes dark, buteo that migrates down from the arctic with Gyrfalcons. Prairie Falcons also looked white sitting on a pole, so, in the early days, we often confused these two species. We wanted to trap Prairie Falcons but not Rough-legged Hawks.

The main trap used for Kestrels, Red-tailed Hawks and other ground hunting, slower-moving raptors on the plains is the 'bal-cha-tri' an Asian device. The word means literally 'horse-hair umbrella' which describes fairly accurately how one is made. The trapper first builds a small wire cage just big enough for one or two mice if you are trapping Kestrels, or big enough for a pigeon or rat if you try for larger raptors. The wire is strong mesh so the quarry inside won't be hurt. In fact, a favourite mouse or pigeon loses its fear of raptors and, instead of freezing when the raptor flies over or onto the trap, continues to move around the cage . The 'bal-cha-tri' is weighted on the bottom with a horseshoe or some other metal and it can have runners on the bottom made from coat hangers. This allows you to set the trap onto the road from a moving car so it slides off onto the shoulder. The illusion, then, is that a car drives past a raptor on a pole and, because the trap is set down from the passenger-side door, the raptor sees a mouse or pigeon suddenly appear across the road in the grass. The raptor doesn't realise that it can't get through the wire so it lands on top of the trap, which has monofilament fishing line (which has replaced horsehair) nooses tied to it. These nooses entangle the raptor's feet without causing it harm. That's the theory anyway and it works better on some days than on others.

The most effective trap used with larger falcons that stoop at prey and strike it at speed is the 'dho-gaza'. A piece of mist-net about 1.5 metres square with washers tied in each corner is fixed to poles with alligator clips so the net detaches from the poles when hit by an attacking falcon. A starling, pigeon or sparrow is tethered on the other side of the net. When the falcon sees the tethered prey it flies from its perch at speed to catch the bird. The falcon hurtles just over the pigeon in an effort to get it to fly upwards where it will be caught in mid-air. The falcon hits the net which detaches from the poles and entangles it.

Describing one of our trips may help you understand the passion we had for these weekends. At dawn we drive out through white snow on open plains dotted with sagebrush and poplar trees. The sky is bright blue without clouds, the air is dry, clean and icy cold. We pass, in the old Chevy, down through Kahlotus and Washtucna and during the first hour see three Red-tailed Hawks and two Rough-legged Hawks on telephone poles and some Northern Harriers and Kestrels in flight. Because these species don't interest us we slow down to identify them and accelerate past. High on a hill to our right we see a bright white raptor perched upright on a telephone pole crossarm. We put the binoculars on it and see a Prairie Falcon, and drive on down the road so it won't fly. We park about 500 metres down the road from the falcon and feel the level of excitement rise in us, excitement that could cause us to make mistakes. We take the poles and mist-net from the back seat. In full view of the falcon, we force the poles into the ground, unfold the mist-net and attach each corner to the alligator clips on the poles. But we're in too much of a hurry and pull the poles too far apart. The net springs from the poles and entangles the washers from each corner. It's a mess that costs us time as we cut the washers off and retie them. The falcon waits patiently. Finally with the net up, we tie a string to one bottom corner leading to a wooden drag that slows the trapped falcon after it hits the net. Next we take the pigeon from its box and place it on the other side of the net. The net stands between the falcon and the pigeon. The pigeon is tethered to a weight by a strap (jess) on one leg so it can flap around but can't get close to the net and tangle itself.

We're all set. After checking everything, we climb back into the Chevy and drive 200 metres down the road away from the trap and the falcon. Then we wait. For 10 minutes the falcon sits quietly. It looks uninterested. Suddenly it bolts off the pole flying straight and hard at the pigeon. The pigeon begins to flap madly as the falcon, flying a direct slanted line, closes in at blistering speed. The falcon hits the net hard, entangles itself and rolls over harmlessly in the sagebrush. We speed up to the trap as fast as the Chevrolet can go, leap out of the car, and rush over to the falcon. We untangle her from the net, a beautiful sandy, white creature with coal black eyes. She's strong and perfect and totally defiant.

In those first trapping days nothing excited us as much as a white Prairie Falcon flying or sitting on a pole and we usually drove off the road or stopped and slammed the car into reverse to get a good view and set the 'dho-gaza' or other trap. Once, seeing a falcon that we thought was our first Gyrfalcon, we stopped the car in such excitement that nothing around us mattered. I slammed the old Chevrolet into reverse and skidded backwards at speed to get a better view when suddenly a car honked behind me and Alan yelled "Stop!". I looked behind us and saw that I'd nearly backed into a State Patrol car, stopping only 6 inches from their bumper. As we expected, the officer came up to the window to have a serious discussion about my driving, why I chose to speed backwards into a police car. Alan, though younger than me, was both smoother and more eloquent when dealing with authority. He talked our way out of the confrontation in less than five minutes, and he seemed to have the officers interested in falcon trapping when he finished.

The first Prairie Falcon trapped that year was a passage female, a falcon hatched that spring, that I took to Roslyn. I walked her every night in the dark after work and can still feel the crunch of very cold snow under my boots, the hairs freezing in my nose and the warm, sweet breath that vaporised from the frightened falcon. Each night we walked in the dark, practiced hooding and finally she fed on my fist and flew to me on a line under the street lights.

During this winter of 1969-70 I met Les Boyd. At a time when Peregrines were revered as the ultimate falconer's bird, and far superior to Prairie Falcons, Les consistently and quietly won falconry meets with Prairie Falcons that outflew Peregrines. He was revered because of his kindness, his commitment to raptor conservation and because he seemed to understand the psychology of falcons better than anyone.

In January 1970 I enrolled at Washington State University at Pullman where Les worked and lived.

3 Pullman

Pullman Washington lies in the Palouse, a region of steep rolling grassland hills. The Nez Pierce Indians bred Appaloosa horses there. Chief Joseph, the most famous Nez Pierce, led his people on a brilliant tactical retreat up to the Canadian border before he and his people were caught by the U.S. Army. It was Chief Joseph who said, "I will fight no more forever" after that retreat. The grasslands in the Palouse may be the richest agricultural lands in the U.S. so it's not surprising that almost everything you see is cultivated. Almost nothing is natural so it seemed an odd place for such a gifted falcon expert to live. Les was raised in the Palouse, he worked there at the university and owned land. But also it was a good area to hunt Hungarian Partridges, pheasants and ducks with falcons.

Falconry

Falconers hunt mainly in autumn and winter because raptors moult in spring and summer. To control the falcon when it hunts, the falconer controls its weight through careful feeding and this is hard to do when the falcon needs to be fat to grow new feathers in spring and summer. In addition, many falconers' birds are used for captive breeding in spring and their progeny aren't ready for training until late summer.

Much of the quarry sought by falconers is introduced or exotic species like European Starlings though some of these, like Ring-necked Pheasants and Hungarian Partridges, are managed as game birds. Falcons use a number of hunting strategies, sometimes flying fast and low over contoured ground to surprise prey and at other times they fly from a high perch, like a cliff, to intercept flying prey. But most falconers try to engineer flights that use another hunting strategy, the vertical or angled stoop where the falcon strikes the quarry hard enough to disable or kill it. If the blow doesn't kill, the falcon quickly separates neck vertebrae with its beak using a special 'tomial tooth' in the upper mandible. Because falcons killed their prey 'humanely', medieval falconers considered them 'noble'. Hawks or eagles that tore at their prey and ate it without first killing it through a bite on the neck were 'ignoble'.

Falcons hunt co-operatively with other falcons and use other animals to flush prey for them. Humans also hunt co-operatively. From this innate behaviour in two species develops a sort of understanding between the falcon and the falconer. The falcon understands that the human partner will assist its hunting. The falconer is rewarded by watching, hearing and feeling a hunt at close hand.

Non-falconers often don't understand the obsession that some have with this form of hunting but it's easier to understand when you see what the falcons can do. This doesn't necessarily justify falconry and there remains considerable opposition to it in North America and Europe and falconry is illegal in countries like Australia, New Zealand, Norway and Sweden.

The ground falconers hunt in Pullman is steep rolling hills lying fallow in winter, with tussocks of last year's wheat and other crops pushing through the snow and soil. Rows of Hawthorn bushes, some large as trees, some smaller, divide fields and intersect roads. We set out on a cold afternoon an hour before sundown walking over the frozen Palouse ground with a male Prairie Falcon on the falconer's fist. The falcon is hooded so he can't see quarry that would distract him and he can't be frightened by animals or cars. Hoods calm even wild-caught, untamed falcons. Freezing gusts of wind blow up every few minutes and the falcon is blown backwards or forwards but quickly regains his balance. It's a dilemma for him - if he spread his wings to re-balance himself, which is the natural thing for him to do, his wings catch the wind and he is further unbalanced. He has learned to keep his balance, as we walk through the rough ploughed stubble, by spreading his wings as little as possible and crouching low on the falconer's glove. After 30 minutes we struggle over the top of a steep hill and see a flock of some five hundred Common Starlings wheeling around the Hawthorn bushes below us. They might roost there. We can't let the starlings see the flash of the falcon's wing because they, the starlings, will fly higher in the sky or seek the shelter of foliage in high trees if they realise the imminent danger. We want them to stay near these low bushes and take refuge there. Then we can flush them out of the bushes with the falcon high above so he can stoop into the flock. This is the essence of Western (as opposed to Arab or Eastern) falconry and is very difficult to organise. Much of our success depends on how fast and strong the falcon looks to the starlings when we remove his hood and release him. If they sense he can outfly them, the starlings will take refuge in the low bushes. If the starlings sense they can outfly the falcon, they will rise up in a cloud and stay above him or fly to cover.

We unhood the falcon and he blinks and looks around. His black pupils dilate and contract as he adjusts to the bright sunlight on snowy ground dotted with wheat stubble. He is a delicate sandy on the back with a white breast covered with dark teardrops and sharp pointed wings crossed high above his tail. He is perfect. The wind is at our back so the falcon can use it to assist his speed. He's ready to fly. The starlings continue to wheel over the bushes. With a forward push of the falconer's hand that signals he is free, we start the flight. The falcon sees the starlings and flies straight for them, closing the 300 metres to the flock with blistering speed. The flight looks to be a failure as the Starlings rise up high in a tight swirling ball and start to rise above the falcon into the dark blue sky tinged by the orange sun to our west. But some twenty lose their nerve as the falcon closes in and they wheel back around and crash into the low Hawthorn bush in a hard black swarm.

It takes only a minute for us to run down the hill to the bush and the falcon, by this time, has started to ring up high in the sky above us. He knows he can use the force of gravity to overcome these starlings but only if he has height when the starlings are flushed. He continues upwards until he is only the size of a fly. The starlings, in the meantime, are squeaking in the bushes like little rusty gates, calling in mass fear, and looking skywards to the falcon, then, across to us, the approaching humans. They are caught in a dilemma but decide to stay, even though humans stand only three metres away. They sense that the alternative, leaving the bush to escape us and try to dodge the hunting falcon, is far too dangerous. We move closer and can almost touch the starlings with a stick when they explode out of the bush, their wings roaring and squawking and we can't hear anything but this deafening escape as they try to reach more bushes just over the hill. We share, with the falcon, a rush of adrenalin. Looking up we see the falcon roll over, close its wings and stoop hard and fast downward. He is a slanting black scratch down the sky as the flock wheels back and tries to regain cover. The falcon cuts downward through the black swirling mass against the darkening blue, we hear a solid, hard thump and see him strike a starling hard on the back and grasp it. A puff of feathers floats down to our right as the falcon carries the starling in a slanted glide down to the marbled snowy soil. The starling has been killed by the impact. As we move closer there is some worry that he'll fly and carry the starling over the hill instead of returning it to us. If we can't retrieve the falcon, he might spend the night out. But he flies up from the ground with the starling to the falconer's glove and takes a reward of a fresh Coturnix quail. The falcon now is panting less and showing less excitement than a few minutes before. Talking excitedly of the hunt, we amble back to the house with the falcon eating on the fist.

Falconers visited Les from Washington and all over the West to learn about the psychology of falcons through the way he handled them and the success that followed. He taught by example, by showing kindness and patience and never using force. Tom Cade, the eminent raptor biologist, told me once that Les was so good with falcons because he had "really good hands". This was true but his gifts were complex. Money came second, or maybe last. Generosity to people, the falcons and the environment came first and how you ordered these priorities showed very much what you were.

Lebarge

In June 1971 Les and I travelled north along the Alcan Highway to Lake Lebarge. A fairly bad storm blew up as we crossed the lake so we pulled the canoe and kayak into Richthoffen Island and spent the night there. This was the island where, before they disappeared, Jake and George used to bury their fish. The next morning we arrived at John's cabin. It was perfect but empty. I had hoped John and Les could meet on the lake but it wasn't to be. I never learned what happened to John.

The following day we went looking for nests of Northern Goshawks. These goshawks followed Bergman's rule. That is, they had larger bodies and proportionally shorter toes than their counterparts down in the warmer mountains of Washington or California. They were adapted to the cold and we wanted to see how they compared to goshawks from down south. Les had broken his ankle just before the trip and had worried about crossing Lake Lebarge with a cast on his foot. I assured him that if the canoe turned over, the water would kill him in five minutes anyway but he didn't seem to be listening and cut the cast off before we crossed. Les could only travel the rough ground on crutches so he stayed near the cabin. Late that day I found a giant nest up the hill from the cabin in a medium-sized Aspen. Lebarge is so far north that trees tended to be short - only about 50 feet high. The nest would be a moderately easy climb.

Les pushed uphill on his crutches through the open park-
land to the bench high above the cabin. The summer sun
heated him so he rested in the cool grass under the nest. He
looked through binoculars at the two four-week-old male
goshawk nestlings as I shinned 30 feet up to the first branch.

Suddenly the adult female crashed in through the foliage
from my right and struck me with force that nearly dislodged me. Les shouted at the hawk and even threw some
sticks while I tucked my face into my left arm for protection
and, with my right, held onto the tree. But she slammed
into me four or five more times. Unlike most attacking
raptors, she hit me in the face as well as the back, and she
tried to strike under my arm at my eyes. Usually if you look
at an attacking raptor, face it, the bird veers off from its
attack. But she didn't follow the rules and, instead, kept
hitting me hard in the face. I could only hold on. Cowed,
and with a bloodied face, I slid down the tree and we re-
treated.

In Europe these goshawks never attack humans at the nest
and, when humans approach, slip away. This is a reaction
to centuries of persecution, persecution so brutal that game-
keepers shot Northern Goshawks completely out of Britain. They have been re-released in numbers in Britain,
mostly from escaped falconer's birds, and now breed there
again. But, even if the persecution stops, I suspect they'll
remain shy for many generations. They won't reach the level
of ferocity we saw on Lebarge.

Prairie Falcons

In June 1972 we banded one of our last broods of Prairie
Falcons in an old raven's nest on a cliff down near Palouse
Falls, Washington. It has to be said that we drank too much
on the drive there and walked rather clumsily on the rough
ground between the cliffs above us and the river below. Because this particular female had a reputation for attacking
humans, we kept a watch skyward. Les had with him a small
bag in addition to the rope and banding equipment but he
didn't say what it contained. Suddenly, as we approached

the nest cliff, the air exploded with the 'cac-cac-cac' alarm call of a defending falcon. She stooped hard from two hundred metres up and we felt the wind from her wings. When I turned to talk to Les, he had dipped into his bag and pulled out a metal hardhat, the kind you see on construction sites, with LES written in large red letters across the front. He looked rather sheepish and self conscious but he quickly pulled it onto his head and crouched low in the sagebrush as the falcon positioned her next attack. As I pointed at Les and laughed at his lack of manliness, the falcon rolled over, singled me out and stooped in a hard downward slant with air rushing through her closed wings and hit me hard on the side of the head. I rolled to the ground and cowered in the sagebrush while Les looked bemused and invulnerable, which, it turned out, he was.

Older nestling falcons, and other raptors, can leap and glide some distance if you climb into their nest. They haven't flown before but they try to fly rather than stay in the nest with you. We were inexperienced in those days about 'premature fledging', not clear about how late we could band these nestlings without running the risk of them jumping. The four females in the nest were about four weeks old but the single male was older or had developed faster. He leapt out as I roped into the nest and glided across the Palouse River. We marked the spot for Les to retrieve him. After banding his four sisters, I climbed back up the rope and went looking for the nestling falcon. After wading across the Palouse River and searching for two hours, we finally found him. We waded back across the river, walked to the top of the cliff and roped down to place him back in the nest. As I climbed back up the rope, he flew out of the nest and across the river again.

Parent falcons will feed their young on the ground and researchers even tether young hawks or eagles onto platforms lower down a tree so they can study feeding behaviour. But we worried about coyotes, which were common there, and knew it was our responsibility to retrieve him. It was dusk but we waded across the river and managed to find him a second time and, just on dark, place him back in the nest. He stayed.

That should be the end of the story but, when we got home and looked in the banding bag, the string of bands for Prairie Falcons was gone. I had left them in the Prairie Falcon eyrie. There probably were other words to describe our performance so far but gross incompetence was the first that came to mind. We now had to get the bands back and avoid causing the male to jump again. We decided that, if we visited the nest after a few days wait, the male might fly strongly and be safe, but his sisters, which develop more slowly, would stay in the nest. We arrived four days later and the male was gone, but the nest on the cliff had partially fallen away and the rest would fall soon. The four remaining females huddled on a narrow ledge and they would certainly fall if we left them.

Les had been working for some time on an idea. Breeding falcons in captivity was in its infancy and most captive females layed infertile eggs; the males didn't do their part. Les would try to get male falcons to contribute semen, voluntarily, to a person and use this to artificially inseminate females. He would imprint males to humans so they wanted to copulate with a special hat Les devised. After he successfully developed this idea, Les received awards and was asked to present his findings at the *Zoological Society in London* and publish in the *Symposium of the Society* and the *Journal of Wildlife Management*. But that was a long way off and, at that time, we talked about the first stage of the project and whether to take Prairie Falcons for a trial. We removed the two largest females from the site with the falling nest to leave more room for the remaining two females. Then, from another nest, we took a male young enough to imprint to Les, that is, he would see Les as his mate. These would be the first nestlings he used in his artificial insemination research. Les developed techniques that were later used by many falcon breeders, including the Peregrine Fund which released captive-bred Peregrines into the wild throughout the U.S. Les directly and indirectly helped the Peregrine regain its former numbers in North America.

When I ran out of money and had no means of support for the last semester, Les gave me a room in his house and free board so I could finish. He never asked anything in return. We often talked during that time about Australia and the raptors there. Books showed six species of falcons, a pure white goshawk and an unstudied population of Peregrines. In 1972, a scout from Australia travelled through Washington and Oregon recruiting teachers for South Australian schools. That summer, with a job waiting in Australia, I visited Lebarge one last time while Les cared for his falcons back in Pullman.

Jerry Olsen

4 Nesting Around Port Augusta

The first things you notice coming into Sydney Airport are thousands of red rooftops near white beaches and the Sydney Harbour Bridge. In September 1972 the Sydney Opera House hadn't been finished. The contrast in climate between Alaska and Sydney wasn't great. The Alaskan summer, in fact, was warmer. But the teaching job was in Port Augusta in South Australia and this looked like nothing in Alaska. The town exists because of a coal-burning electricity generating powerhouse and a railways repair and maintenance centre. Almost all roofs are galvanised, corrugated iron that dazzles in the blistering heat and sun. The countryside is saltbush and bluebush on red sand with creeks dominated by huge eucalypt trees. When it was really hot, and it got to 120 degrees Fahrenheit there, the eucalypt trees smelled medicinal, but good, mixed with the tang of sea air. Except for the eucalypt and acacia trees it was like sagebrush country in Washington state.

Behind Port Augusta stand the Flinders Ranges, a dry, rocky set of mountains stretching north-east from the ocean at Spencer's Gulf. Peregrine Falcons nested in the rocky gorges of these ranges and Kestrels, Hobbies, Black, Peregrine and Brown Falcons nested in eucalypt trees in the creeks that poured out of the mountains. The plains north-west of Port Augusta are dry and sometimes dominated by red sand and acacia trees. It's like Africa, even Ostriches live there, a remnant population released from captivity after the feather trade collapsed. South-east of the ranges, and the town, lies an island of arable farmland near Melrose and Wilmington where thousands of Galahs and Corellas gather around wheat crops. Later we would hunt there.

Looking back now it is easy to forget how little was known about Australian raptors in 1972. The major studies by David Baker-Gabb, Nick Mooney, Tom Aumann, Clayton White, Penny Olsen, Bill Emison, Stephen Debus, Greg Czechura and others were some years off. Because birds had been wrongly typed and sexed in museums and much of the raptor knowledge was based on shooting raptors and preparing skins from them, there were gaps and there was misinformation. So we tried to find out the basics - how many Peregrines lived around Port Augusta? What did they eat? Did Peregrines catch the same prey as the Black Falcons? How did their hunting strategies compare? Were falcons near Port Augusta declining from pesticide use as they were elsewhere in the world? Terry Dennis, the ranger at Alligator Gorge National Park between Port Augusta and Wilmington, helped to address these questions. He and Helen and their three children lived at the ranger's headquarters at Alligator Gorge right above a Peregrine eyrie. They were, and are, honest and generous people who always gave more than they took.

To understand the biology of falcons around Port Augusta we started with basics. Individuals of each species try to get their genes into future generations by harnessing energy. To do this they need to survive and ensure that their progeny survive. They need shelter and water, though some raptors obtain enough water from their food. Most importantly, the thing that differentiates one raptor species from another, is foraging - the manner in which they gather food. So learning what prey each species hunted and how they hunted it could help us understand how each species survived and bred.

In the beginning, we had to find nests of falcons - Peregrines, Blacks, Hobbies, Kestrels and Brown Falcons. So we started to drive and walk through the Flinders Ranges and explore the thin lines of trees pouring out of the ranges along intermittent creeks. Hopefully, the experience with Prairie Falcons and goshawks in North America could help.

We started our search on Stirling Creek, a large creek with giant Red Gums, that flowed straight from the ranges for ten kilometres before it widened to a floodplain 200 metres wide at the railway township of Sterling North near Port Augusta. Here, during September, we walked for hours up the creek and back down and found our first raptor nests. The creek was rich. Birds of some sort, especially Galahs and other bright parrots, nested every few metres and certain raptors were common. Black Kites, Whistling Kites, Kestrels, Brown Goshawks, Collared Sparrowhawks, Little Eagles and Brown Falcons all nested on Stirling Creek.

River Red Gums are tall with wide bases and slippery grey and white bark that makes them dangerous to climb. We had to learn how to reach the topmost branches and engineer our way up the huge trunks without falling. Every tree differed and presented new problems. We threw ropes up over the lower branches, sometimes fifty feet up, then pulled ourselves up, hand over hand, to embrace a giant limb with our face against the trunk. Then we might use a 'sloth manoeuvre' - hang upside down from the limb, with hands and feet wrapped around it, hook one foot against the trunk and lever ourself up onto the limb. Otherwise we might chin up on the limb and flip ourselves up onto it, land stiff-armed on the branch and throw a leg over and sit. We then stood on that limb and threw the rope over the next good limb and, thus, worked our way up the tree. After time, we developed a feel for which limbs would or wouldn't hold our weight and which were too big for us to reach around with arms and legs. Slipping off a large limb at these heights would be fatal. Stirling Creek and its powerful white trees held us captive and we were driven to find all the raptors there.

But the main quest was for falcons, especially Peregrines. In Britain and North America Peregrines were declining and, in the United States, became extinct east of the Mississippi River. In the 1960's Derek Ratcliffe was hired by the Nature Conservancy in Britain to investigate reports that Peregrine numbers were increasing and killing more racing pigeons particularly in the South Wales mining valleys which were long a stronghold of fanciers. Not only did he find that Peregrines were declining, not increasing at all, but, in Peregrines he observed, saw some odd things. He found crushed eggs in nests and he saw some falcons eating their own eggs.

In his search for answers to these questions, he examined eggs that were taken from Peregrine nests early in the century through to the 1960's. Egg collecting was a popular hobby in Britain and Peregrines had lovely, reddish marbled eggs that were favourites to collect. Oologists drilled a small hole in the egg and blew the contents out. The remaining shell was stored and could be saved indefinitely. Derek realized he could contrast the thickness of eggs in these early collections with those in later collections and to eggs from nests he studied. To do this, he developed a simple, but elegant, formula - **weight** of the eggshell divided by **width** of the eggshell times **length** of the eggshell, that is, **wt/width x length** of the eggshell. He found that eggs taken before DDT was introduced to Britain, around 1945, had thicker shells and were more able to withstand incubation, the female sitting on them and rolling them periodically, than eggs taken after DDT was introduced. Thin eggs broke under the weight of the incubating female and she sometimes ate them.

Though Rachel Carson had written *Silent Spring* by that time, and some people were expressing concern about pesticides, the evidence showing how pesticides harmed wildlife just wasn't there. What we take for granted today, that chlorinated hydrocarbons like DDT, its metabolite DDE, dieldrin, heptachlor epoxide and other chemicals remained in the environment for years and continued to harm wildlife, was not widely accepted. Consequently, pesticide companies continued to manufacture DDT and other chemicals and agriculturists spread them through the environment. Derek Ratcliffe's work and the Peregrine became important in this controversy because he was the first person to publish evidence that DDT thinned eggshells and this evidence was first shown for the Peregrine. As it turned out, many other birds like some ducks, show no dramatic eggshell thinning after they ingest DDT so chemical companies argued for some time that DDT did no harm. Even some raptor species bred with no apparent effects in areas of high DDT use. But this was because the main raptor species affected by DDT, and more toxic chemicals like dieldrin, ate birds and large fish. These pesticides concentrate over time. Bird prey, on the whole, lives longer than insect or mammal prey and, therefore, concentrates more pesticides in each body. In addition, many birds are insectivorous instead of herbivorous, so the pesticides are concentrated, multiplied by this extra trophic level. Raptors that ate rabbits, ground squirrels and other short-lived herbivores would ingest lesser amounts of pesticides than those that ate longer-lived birds, especially insectivorous birds. Some twenty years later Derek visited Australia to compare Australian Peregrines with those he knew in Britain.

Peregrine nest sites affected by pesticides in Britain and North America were gradually abandoned. But this pattern was only evident if individual territories were watched over a long period of time. Peregrines don't necessarily fledge young every year and sometimes they won't attend the nest site closely in years when they have no young. The researchers won't see the adults. Consequently, it's difficult to tell whether the site is abandoned or whether the adults are, simply, less visible because they have no eggs or young holding them to the site. The pattern of territories gradually abandoned that Derek found in Britain and Joseph Hickey and Tom Cade found in North America could be the pattern in Australia. If we found some Peregrine and other bird-eating falcons nesting, and checked these territories through several years, we could learn whether falcons around Port Augusta were disappearing. In addition we could gather infertile eggs from nests, locate egg collections with old eggs and compare shell thickness from pre-DDT to post-DDT eggs. As it turned out, Peregrines were affected by pesticides and eggshell thinning in certain areas only, and, around Port Augusta, were fairly free from the effects of eggshell thinning.

Falcons don't build their own nests; they have to use a ledge or pothole on a cliff, a tree cavity or the nest of another bird like a hawk, eagle or crow. We started to search Alligator Gorge National Park in the Flinders Ranges just east of Port Augusta. This forested region has sandstone cliffs along several creeks that drain nearby high country. A number of the cliffs had 'whitewash' on them which could be Peregrine droppings. Each of these cliffs was checked by climbing down a polypropylene or hemp rope, hand over hand, with no equipment in those days, to check ledges or splashes of whitewash. Finally, after five days searching the park from Mambray Creek north-east to Alligator Gorge, I climbed down the rope to a ledge on a 10 metre cliff along the upper reaches of Alligator Creek. A large female Peregrine burst out from the ledge and flew away cacking loudly. I was surprised at how stocky she looked as she flew away, like a very fat duck. The nest ledge was empty but had been used. Prey remains from Galahs and other parrots littered the ledge and young may have fledged that year. With this first nest, and those that followed, we could study the pattern, the types of cliffs, countryside, prey and terrain where we might find more.

Two weeks later we found our first Black Falcon and Australian Hobby nests on Spear Creek, near Stirling Creek. But while searching for a second Peregrine site in Warrens Gorge I slipped and fell, breaking my ankle. Medical help could be primitive in Port Augusta and the ankle, though broken, wasn't x-rayed and was misdiagnosed. It slowed our progress that year and was a nuisance until, nearly 20 years later, the bone splinters were removed.

In the following year, 1973, we found more Peregrine, Black Falcon and Hobby nests and began to band and measure young and collect prey remains. Peregrines near their nests would attack us but actual nest ledges could be hard to find on big cliffs. However, some females tended to dip into a site with one wing and this inadvertently signalled the nest location. Other falcons usually nested in trees and, some, like Black Falcons and Kestrels, successfully laid eggs and raised young in the abandoned nests of ravens high up in the structure of electricity pylons. There seemed to be no protection there from the sun but, when we climbed these nests, we found the angle braces offered more shade than expected.

Galahs showed up more often in prey remains than other bird prey and Peregrines and Black Falcons certainly killed many in the nearby wheatfields and eucalypt-lined creek beds. They, and Little Corellas, were some of the largest prey taken and more obvious in the remains gathered from nests. We also found Mallee Ring-necks, Fairy Martins, Budgerigars, Blue Bonnets, European Starlings, honeyeaters and other smaller prey that also played a part in their diet.

We made inroads into the egg-collecting community, beginning with Tom Brandon in Wilmington and his friend Gordon Ragless of Adelaide, to compare pre-DDT and post-DDT eggs from the area. Members of this secret society, and many had to remain secret because egg collecting without a permit was illegal, were reluctant to show us their collections. Only a few had permits. But, with time, they trusted us and allowed access to their giant hardwood cabinets filled with rows of beautiful eagles', hawks' and falcons' eggs. One collector hid his cabinets behind a secret wall built into his house. The obsession, the detail they had in notes and records about each clutch, the nest, species, location and all they thought important, stunned us. They treasured these collections because the collections showed their life's work, lifted them above the ordinary. They traded rare clutches and notes and proudly showed and bargained their exacting work.

Ten years later the Parks and Wildlife authorities in each state began to confiscate their collections and threaten prosecution to those who resisted the raids or continued to collect eggs without a permit. Some turned their friends in, others became distrustful of everyone and became total recluses. Certain collectors were said to have smashed their collections, decades of meticulous work, so the authorities couldn't take them. It was a hard time for them and many felt persecuted. But many collections did go to museums where the painstaking work could be used. The egg-collecting network died in the 1980's and some kept their secrets in retaliation for what, they thought, authorities and some professional ornithologists had done to them.

Other basic information was gathered on falcons. Black and Peregrine Falcons near Port Augusta are about the same size. Females weighed about 950 grams and males weighed about 650 grams. Black Falcons didn't have yellow feet and didn't scream as they attacked prey as was depicted in books and articles. Peregrines had clutch sizes of about three and brood sizes of about two. Black Falcons had clutch sizes of about four and brood sizes of about three. So mortality must be higher for Black Falcons than Peregrines and compensated by larger brood sizes in Black Falcons.

The Peregrines had a darker, more complete helmet on their head, perhaps for reducing glare in bright sunlight, than Peregrines in Europe or North America. They were more solidly built with more body muscle, shorter legs (tarsus) and a heavier beak than most other Peregrines. These may be adaptations for catching Galahs and other parrots that are notoriously hard to kill and, if they aren't dispatched quickly, can damage a falcon with their heavy beaks. Peregrines had the typical hard feathers of other Peregrines around the world that allowed them to slip through the air without resistance and gives them a duck-like waterproofing. Though Peregrines live in arid Australia, and even on Uluru (Ayers Rock) in the centre of Australia, they're not really heat adapted. Desert Peregrines seemed to be recent arrivals from a wetter, more temperate climate and they survived in deserts by nesting near water, hunting during the coolest part of the day and nesting and roosting in the cool protection of shaded rock. They overheated and tired easily when they hunted in hot weather.

In contrast, Black Falcons were heat adapted so they could perch out in hot, direct sun that would kill a Peregrine. They hunted in heat and soared for long periods on thermals. Early writers compared them to frigatebirds and greatly admired their endurance on the wing. Though Black Falcons weighed about the same as Peregrines, they had softer feathers and longer wings and tails. So they had a lower wing loading than Peregrines and more agility and capacity to soar. A Black Falcon could stoop from height onto a rabbit or ground bird but a Peregrine might strike the ground or bushes if it tried such a manoeuvre. Black Falcons seemed to be nomadic or partially migratory and, after they bred each year, followed quail from the hot north to the cooler south. In summer they could often be seen on farmland near Adelaide. The Black Falcon was more aggressive and willing to attack larger prey than was the Peregrine. They often robbed Peregrines and we thought that many of the Galah remains found in Black Falcons' nests had been stolen from Peregrines. In that respect they resembled the Saker, another desert falcon.

We had two and a half good years on Stirling Creek and the surrounding countryside. They've killed Stirling Creek now. Mining for the crusher there exposes the roots of the giant trees. Giant River Red Gum trees on the lower reaches have died and the kites, eagles, hawks and falcons no longer nest there. There is no regeneration of young trees because saplings are eaten by sheep and cattle and salt levels have risen. When the old trees die, the creek will be finished for breeding raptors. Perhaps this feeling of loss over disappearing creeks, trees and raptors that lived there is part of living in times of progress. It also unites us as conservationists.

5 Hunting Around Port Augusta

As mentioned in Chapter 4, the most important thing to differentiate one raptor species from another is their hunting style. They find a niche by hunting prey that other predators don't hunt, often in a different way from the way other predators hunt. Many falcons hunt the most dangerous prey of all, flying birds. The falcon takes risks to catch these birds by flying at speed, sometimes close to cover or through flocks, so collision with trees, bushes, the ground or the prey occurs. These collisions can be fatal if the falcon injures a wing and can't hunt. So, by learning something about how these falcons hunted, we learned about the species.

Falconry as a sport was and is illegal in Australia but various wildlife authorities allow raptors to be flown for scientific work, for wildlife films and for rehabilitation. Many falconers in countries where falconry is legal argue that falconers do a lot of good for the birds. Australian authorities, in a sense, agree. They try to ensure, before permits are given, that people who have raptors in captivity are doing some good for the birds. In 1973 the National Parks and Wildlife Service in South Australia gave us permission to train and use two falcons - a Peregrine we called Elizabeth and a Black Falcon we called Mary.

Both species regularly caught birds, but Peregrines and Black Falcons hunted differently and we learned more about these differences from the two trained falcons. Elizabeth was taken from an eyrie in the Flinders Ranges near Wilmington when she was about four weeks old. Mary was a wild-caught, first-year Black Falcon. She came from a bird bander in South Australia who used padded rabbit traps to catch raptors at a pigeon barn. Numbers of the falcons he trapped were injured, including this Black Falcon so, technically, she was a falcon undergoing rehabilitation. I took the bander some proper noose traps, asked him not to use the rabbit traps again and sent two of his injured raptors to an Adelaide veterinarian. As I didn't want the bander in trouble, I didn't reveal his name. In 1974 this event turned very sour as I was blamed for injuring the falcons and my permits to keep raptors were revoked until the problem was resolved.

At any rate, two falcons, the Black Falcon and the Peregrine, were trained and released at separate times in open areas near Port Augusta and Wilmington to compare their hunting styles.

Comparing Black Falcons and Peregrines

As Elizabeth, the Peregrine, was fed largely on Galahs while she was in the nest, it wasn't surprising that she wanted to hunt Galahs when she started to fly. We drove the dusty back roads near Wilmington until we saw flocks of cockatoos feeding in grain fields. The car was stopped and the Peregrine carried from the car and released towards them. Mary flew directly at the Galahs and Little Corellas, very low and fast so they didn't see her silhouette against the sky. But often they seemed to have 'guard birds' posted in nearby trees, or on fence posts, that warned those feeding on the ground that a Peregrine was coming. The cockatoos, and there could be thousands of birds in each flock, would explode upwards, just as she arrived, in a great splash of pink, grey and white against the green hills and blue sky. The noise of thousands of screeching Galahs and Little Corellas deafened us.

Sometimes she caught one just as it rose from the ground. But other times she speared through the flock at great speed and the flock mushroomed further skywards like a pink, white and grey nuclear bomb. If the Galahs and corellas got above her, she tail-chased them and these flights could ring up several hundred metres before she would then stoop, flying towards the earth, and try to strike the prey in mid-air. When she caught one, either as they rose or in a stoop, she glided to the ground with it and immediately separated the neck vertebrae with her beak. This prevented the Galah or Little Corella from biting and injuring her with its powerful beak.

With other prey, like Bronze-winged Pigeons, both Mary and Elizabeth would stoop from great heights at the pigeons as they flushed. Mary's stoop was generally more vertical than that of the Peregrine. In fact, we saw her and other Black Falcons stoop from height onto a pigeon, quail or other prey right on the ground. Black Falcons had less powerful direct flight than Peregrines and their weight was lighter in proportion to their body size. They were, consequently, much more agile than Peregrines and could fly in and around cover with less risk of collision. Wild Black Falcons also showed what we thought was considerable intelligence and versatility. One flew 15 metres above a Swamp Harrier that was quartering farmland. It stooped at the harrier each time it tried to get out from under the falcon. It was as if the falcon kept the harrier working for it, kept it marshalling prey for the falcon, and would release the harrier from servitude when the job was done. Black Falcons shepherded flocks of Galahs, flying lazily after them and keeping them in the air. If a Galah lost its nerve and tried to reach cover, the falcon launched an attack towards the prey, a downwards stoop with rapidly beating wings. They also used long tail chases on Feral Pigeons, Crested Pigeons, and Galahs, that seemed to be aimed at wearing these prey down. A number of times we saw them rob other raptors, including Peregrines, and suspected a number of the Galah carcasses we found in Black Falcon nests on the Wilmington and Port Augusta plains had been stolen from Peregrines.

Black Falcons caught Crested Pigeons from a stoop and commonly followed farm machinery, animals, people and even other raptors that might flush prey for them. Mary, and wild Black Falcons, were also insectivorous. They caught grasshoppers and other flying insects on the wing and ate the insect in flight, holding it in their fist like a child eats an ice-cream cone.

Because Black Falcons naturally used mediating agents to flush prey for them, Mary seemed to know, instinctively, the advantages of flying above us, 'waiting-on' in falconry terms. To recount a flight: wild Black Falcons used to come overhead as we approached some empty wells on the Wilmington plains near Hammond. These wells were used by Feral Pigeons that roosted there at night and dove into the wells if a wild falcon came near. We drove down the rutted dirt road towards the wells, with Mary perched on the back seat and bouncing in the ruts, hitting me each time with a sharp wing shot out to retain her balance. The four-wheel drive was parked and Mary lifted from her perch on the back seat and released on the plain.

She flew up, ringing higher and higher above the wells, and levelled of at about 200 feet. We couldn't see her clearly because, looking up at her, we looked into the sun. Black Falcons seem phlegmatic, not excitable like Prairie Falcons or Peregrines, and Mary floated lazily above us as we worked for her. She seemed unconcerned. When she was in position directly above the wells, we walked over and looked in. Five pigeons clung to the dirt walls and looked up at us then at Mary. After a minute, an old male pigeon lost his composure as we stood over him and burst up through the 10 metre wide mouth and out of the well, flew low to the ground at breakneck speed towards the next well some 500 metres away. Mary rolled over from 200 feet up and stooped almost vertically at the pigeon that now was flying only centimetres above the grey saltbush. She struck the pigeon hard on the back. A puff of grey feathers rose from the impact and drifted downwind. She held the pigeon by the shoulders and glided to the ground with it. She killed it immediately, as all falcons do, by separating its neck vertebrae with her beak, then she began to pull feathers out of the pigeon and feed there on the red ground between the sparse grey bushes. Mary kept looking up at us as we watched her because a wild-caught raptor never becomes completely tame, never completely trusts humans. But we knew we were privileged to watch her hunt, and eat, and fortunate to have her teach us.

Conspicuous Prey

Falcons are known to select out conspicuous prey, like birds that look or behave abnormally. For example, they catch a white pigeon from a flock of dark birds. Charles Darwin in *The Origin of Species* counselled pigeon fanciers that "hawks are guided by eyesight to their prey - so much so that on parts of the continent people are warned not to keep white pigeons, as being most liable to destruction". It may not be colour itself but individuality in the flock which draws a hunting falcon to the "odd bird out". Derek Ratcliffe, the eminent British Peregrine expert, believed that this "odd bird out" notion showed how Peregrines, as agents of natural selection, weed out sub-standard individuals in the prey population. The German falconer, Gustl Eutermoster, flew a trained Peregrine at Rooks and shot a similar-sized sample of Rooks at random. Forty percent of the Rooks caught by the falcon were in less than peak condition, including moult or illness, whereas only 23% in the shot sample were so classified.

In the winter of 1973 we compared the Galahs and Little Corellas caught by Mary the Peregrine on the Wilmington plains with those shot from the same flocks with a shotgun (Table 1).

The sample was small but cockatoos caught by Elizabeth weighed less than those shot and a disproportionate number were thin and sick with matting around the vent. We later found this illness to be Ornithosis or 'Parrot Fever', a type of pneumonia that humans can catch from birds. Since Terry and Helen Dennis had kindly kept the sample in their freezer, with their other food, and authorities had passed the story to the newspapers of a 'potential epidemic' raging in the parrots around Port Augusta, we did worry for a while. Our worries proved unfounded.

Table 1   Weights of Galahs and Corellas caught by a trained Peregrine compared with a sample that was shot.

	Peregrine caught	**Shot**
Galahs	236.3 grams (5 birds)	327 grams (5 birds)
Little Corellas	311.7 grams (3 birds)	381.7 grams (3 birds)

We asked Jim Robinson, from Adelaide, to take another small sample, and it was analysed for pesticides. He flushed feral pigeons from a barn under another trained female Peregrine that stooped into the flock. After several days, and a number of flights, the Peregrine caught five pigeons. Using a torch, Jim caught five pigeons from the same barn at night and we compared the five pigeons taken by the falcon to the five taken by hand (Table 2).

As with Galahs and Corellas, the pigeons caught by the falcon weighed less. There appeared to be higher levels of pesticide in the falcon-caught sample. Only the pigeons killed by the falcon contained residues other than DDT or its metabolites - heptachlor epoxide, lindane and dieldrin. In addition, one pigeon killed by the falcon had a fully formed egg in its cloaca. We inferred from these small experiments that trials were worth repeating with larger samples. If the same results occur, and if this pattern exists in the wild, Peregrines may select prey that is somehow encumbered by pesticides because they see differences that humans don't detect. Falcons may eat higher cumulative doses of pesticides than are evident from only sampling their prey because pesticides affect the behaviour of such prey.

In 1990 Robert Kenward reported on trials with trained Northern Goshawks that hunted Wood Pigeons in England. He found that goshawks were less likely to catch defective prey during a surprise attack, when the flock of pigeons saw the hawk only at the last moment. Goshawks were more likely to catch defective prey during prolonged chases, particularly when the goshawk had time to see that certain individuals would be easier quarry.

Table 2   Feral pigeons caught by a Peregrine compared with those caught by hand.

	Peregrine caught (5 pigeons)	Collected by hand from night roost (5 pigeons)
Average Weight	323.8 grams	372.5 grams
Total DDT*	0.9	0.05
Total residues*	0.11	0.05
Sex ratio	M=4, F=1	M=1, F=4

*parts per million wet weight of breast muscle

This sort of work uses captive raptors to help us understand the behaviour of raptors. Hopefully we'll see more of it.

Escape Behaviour

Prey species, like pigeons and cockatoos, use many escape behaviours. For example, they dive for cover into grass, trees and other vegetation and circle high into the air so the falcon can't get above and stoop on them. Some birds, like Feral Pigeons, evolved loose body feathers that pull out easily when a falcon tries to snare them.

Flocking birds, like Common Starlings, group tightly and turn in unison. This not only provides a multitude of targets that confuses the attacking falcon, but makes defective or conspicuous prey easier to see. The falcon can more easily single out and chase these individuals. This flocking behaviour is sometimes termed a "Jonah strategy" because the predator can more easily select a victim while other members of the flock escape and don't waste time or energy defending themselves.

At other times flocking can protect all the individuals in a group. One evening at dusk, we were driving home from studying Peregrines when we saw a male Black Falcon make repeated attacks from a dead tree into and through flocks of Common Starlings. These Starlings continued to pour from the surrounding farmland into a reed bed, all evading the falcon's attack, and settling in the reeds. The falcon missed wildly each time and, to make things worse, a Brown Goshawk, sitting in the same tree, eventually dove into the reed bed, came out with a screeching starling clutched under its tail, and flew away.

The Black Falcon, confused by the co-ordinated, swirling mass of starlings, looked as though it would go hungry. We decided on a rather mean experiment - rush in and flush the starlings from the reed bed so they would rise in a flock, as before. But this time the flock would be unco-ordinated, in fear, because we wouldn't let them settle back into the reed bed. They'd lack the control of perfect unison that, earlier, had so confused the falcon. The starlings rose up in a dark, swirling cloud as we crashed into the reeds and the Black Falcon flew in, taking a starling easily from the mass above our heads. To us it was clear that flocking itself didn't save the starlings from the Black Falcon's earlier attacks. Instead, it was the way the flock was organized and the way it turned in confusing unison that saved them.

Peregrines and Black Falcons are remarkable birds. Mary and Elizabeth helped with one more project, at Mascot Airport, before they went back to the wild. Hopefully, they had a long life.

6 Sydney Airport and Port Lincoln

In December 1973 Peter Slater, the author and artist of *A Field Guide to Australian Birds,* telephoned. He'd been asked by the Department of Civil Aviation to help with a project at Sydney's Mascot Airport where Silver Gulls, and other birds, were a danger to aircraft. The authorities there wanted to try a Peregrine at the airport to see if it would scare birds and, most importantly, to see if the falcon could be controlled and not imperil aircraft. We decided to transport Elizabeth, the Peregrine, to Sydney in February and fly her on the airport.

In Britain, falcons were, at that time, successfully chasing birds from U.S. military air bases. If the trial at Sydney worked, they would bring in British falconers for a larger trial. But the bird problems in Sydney were different from those in Britain and the same techniques that worked so well overseas would have to be modified for Sydney. On the other hand, falcons might not work at all.

The First Sydney Trial

The airport authorities flew Elizabeth and me to Sydney in a Lear jet where we met Peter and could see the bird problem at first hand. In England most bird problems at airports comprised ground-feeding species that landed on air-

45

fields to forage or roost. Some nested there and the danger occurred when these birds rose up and flew in front of a jet as it took off or landed. Jet engines sucked the birds through their intakes, which damaged parts of the motor and, in some cases, stopped the engines and caused aircraft to crash. It was a particularly dangerous problem for single-engined jet fighters. Falcons, the reports claimed, did work successfully on these military bases. On British airfields, they flew falcons or left them out for long periods to chase problem birds away. Because the gulls and other birds so feared the falcon, and didn't want to be under a flying, hunting falcon, they left the airport.

But Sydney turned out to be very different. A number of species, particularly Silver Gulls, had, for decades, flown south each morning along the New South Wales coast from their roosting and nesting grounds to their feeding grounds and then back north each night. Rubbish tips provided food for the gulls, exacerbating the problem. Then, to make things worse, the government of the day built a new runway to handle increasing air traffic. This runway stretched east-west, across the existing north-south runway and out into Sydney Harbour on a giant, artificial rock peninsula. Ornithologists, like Gerry van Tets from the CSIRO Division of Wildlife Research, warned this runway would create a problem because gulls and other birds travelled north-south up and down the coast and would continue to do so. That's exactly what happened. Twice a day they would cross this new peninsula supporting the east-west runway. Twice a day flocks of gulls and other birds flew over the runway about 100 feet up in front of passenger jets as they took off and landed.

For us, as we stood on the runway and looked up at these gulls and jets using the same airspace, it was a worrying sight. Twice each day during their migration, the Department of Civil Aviation shot many gulls and other birds. This reduced the bird numbers and the danger to aircraft. In addition to shotguns, they also fired star shells or cracker shells up into the flocks, projectiles that exploded near the bird flocks high above the shooters. We watched the gulls fly across the runway at a lower level, then rise to a higher level when the airport vehicles approached. The flocks rose up just out of shotgun range or moved further down the runway and crossed there. The gulls showed great determination to reach their food source in the morning and their homes at night, but they didn't land on the airfield as in Britain. They wouldn't fear a falcon if they could stay above it and they may just fly higher if a falcon was introduced. Unlike the restricted military airfields in Britain, this was a busy domestic airport. So in many ways the bird problems at Sydney differed from those in Britain and, though falcons helped there, Elizabeth might not scare birds at Mascot. To make things worse, Elizabeth had learned to fly in low and fast to hide her outline from Galahs and Corellas. She would fly low under the flocks of Silver Gulls.

Peter Slater and I watched and learned, and discussed how to fly the Peregrine. He's a gentle man who shows great sensitivity and concern for birds. Part of his motivation to help at Mascot was the safety of air passengers but also he felt bad about the shooting of gulls. At one point, while he watched the evening shoot, Peter walked to the shore and picked up a tern that had tumbled from the sky full of shot. He tried to revive it but, after five minutes, it stopped breathing and lay still. Peter expressed sadness over the loss and returned to his room with the dead tern to paint its image on paper before the beak, eye and feet colours faded. We planned, in the morning, to release Elizabeth beside the east-west runway and watch the reaction of bird flocks flying to their feeding grounds.

Before light, we rose, took the Peregrine from her perch in the grassy yard, and climbed into the airport vehicle. The car arrived on the north side of the runway extension about halfway between the coast and the end of the artificial peninsula. As we lifted the Peregrine from the back seat and prepared her to fly, groups of Silver Gulls, five and ten in each band, started to drift in from the north.

We saw some near misses. The Department of Civil Aviation already had picked up a large collection of birds struck by jets at the airport. They analysed the carcasses for species type, age, gut content and other data. Jets hit mostly Silver Gulls, sometimes sucking them into their engines. We saw no actual strikes that morning but authorities assured us that if we stood there long enough we would see a gull and aircraft collide.

As the morning brightened, we watched for the next group of gulls to come. As the gulls approached to within 500 metres, we released Elizabeth. She flew along the side of the runway, low and lazy, over the perimeter fence, out over the sea and coursed around me, down to the lure and not towards the gulls; they didn't look like cockatoos. One group of gulls that had been foraging in the sea just offshore, lifted from the water and flew away calling as she wheeled towards them. Elizabeth gained some height and the flocks that had been crossing the runway about 40 metres up suddenly turned and flew back up the coast. We tried this four or five more times and each group of gulls turned when they saw the Peregrine and flew back towards their roost. But when she came back to the ground, the gulls moved further down the runway to a place where they apparently felt safe and continued to fly over the runway. While she flew, Elizabeth had some effect, but she had no long-term effect after she left the sky.

Peter flew back to his home near Brisbane and the Department of Civil Aviation flew Elizabeth and me back to Port Augusta. We had decided with Peter to try three falcons at the airport in a second trial that winter.

The Second Sydney Trial

We returned in August 1974 with Elizabeth, the Peregrine, Mary the Black Falcon mentioned in Chapter 4 and another Black Falcon, trapped with Mary, Peter trained. We drove out early on a bleak wintry morning to the east-west runway we'd tried before. Fog was thick and jets roared up from the runway out over the sea until only flashing red lights showed through the mist. Peter lifted one Black Falcon from the back seat of the department's four-wheel drive and prepared her to fly. I did the same with Mary. As we watched, groups of Silver Gulls came in from the north, about 40 metres up, and crossed the runway over our heads. At first only the gulls' black wing tips blinked in the gloom because their white bodies were masked by the white fog. But as they came nearer we saw their buoyant forms float above us and underneath the rising jets. We released the two Black Falcons and watched for a reaction. When we flew them at home, these falcons tended to go up and 'wait-on' above us and they did that morning. But the gulls didn't react to the Black Falcons as they did to the Peregrine, they continued to fly on to their feeding grounds. At first this perplexed us because the Black Falcons flew higher and the gulls should have been less secure as the falcons gained height. Silver Gulls near Port Augusta, where Black Falcons are common, plunged into the nearest water and cried in fear anytime Mary drifted near them. But the coastal New South Wales gulls had probably never seen a Black Falcon; the falcon's shape apparently didn't threaten them.

When we flew Elizabeth again she did frighten them even though she skated in low and stayed near us. At one point, a wild Peregrine came in and attacked her which frightened the gulls so much they landed on the sea and stayed there for some 30 minutes after the wild Peregrine left and Elizabeth was grounded. We also tried sequences of deterrents. Elizabeth flew around me and some gulls took refuge offshore in the sea. She was grounded and the airport staff fired a cracker shell at the gulls in the water which caused them to rise up in a flock and Elizabeth was released again. This sequence badly frightened and confused the gulls so they stayed away for nearly an hour.

So we learned a few more things on this second trial but, still, there was no clear way that falcons could be used to deter gulls from Sydney Airport. The Department of Civil Aviation did see potential from the trials and decided to bring to Sydney *Longwings Incorporated,* a British company that specialised in using falcons at airports. We returned home to prepare for the trials with *Longwings* starting in February 1975.

Because Elizabeth and the two Black Falcons would moult in August and continue their moult through March, they couldn't be used in these summer trials, couldn't be flown through the moult. As field trials on other prey species continued near Port Augusta, Elizabeth and Mary soared higher and higher in their hunting flights to put in spectacular stoops at various birds. This type of hunting meant they were more likely to be lost, and both spent nights out when they failed to return from long flights. This happened more and more frequently until, early that spring of 1974, neither returned.

The Port Lincoln Trials

In October we took a male and a female Peregrine nestling from two nests in the Flinders Ranges for the *Longwings* trials in February. I took them south to Port Lincoln to stay and work with Jeff and Anita Jolly. He was, and is, one of our finest raptor experts and he currently works as a wildlife artist in Melrose, South Australia. Port Lincoln, for some reason, was a very small place that produced a lot of strong men, including Dean Lukin the Olympic gold medallist. Jeff was a powerful climber and did many hours of field work on dozens of nests near Port Lincoln. That January and February of 1975 we held trials with the local Silver Gulls and he and Anita generously helped fly the two Peregrines.

Port Lincoln is a beautiful little fishing and holiday town, very different from Port Augusta. The climate is more temperate and summers could be cool. It rained a lot more and tended to stay green in summer. Great White Sharks were common there and the locals who knew the waters well, tended not to swim there.

There was a large tuna processing plant in Port Lincoln that attracted hundreds of gulls to the effluent of fish offal it discharged. Gulls flew daily from their roosts to feed at this plant. We decided to fly the falcons near the sea along the route between the gulls' roosting grounds and the fish processing plant to see if they would change course over time and fly a different route. The scale here was smaller than at Sydney Airport but we thought we could learn from these trials and prepare the two Peregrines to chase gulls in Sydney. Silver Gulls were a natural prey of Peregrines but taken mainly by females in the later half of the nestling period. If these two falcons were fed gulls, or had gull wings and feathers tied to their lure, they eventually would chase them. They did, but only the female was bold enough to chase them hard and actually catch and kill them. The male was intimidated by the gulls' size and threat displays.

At first we flew each Peregrine to the lure as the gulls approached. Though the Peregrines flew in tight, low circles around us, it produced a similar effect to that seen in Sydney. The gulls were initially frightened and flew out to sea where they remained until we brought the falcon down. Then they detoured wide around us and continued down the shore to the fish processing plant. In these lure-flying trials the gulls feared the male more than the female, we guessed, because he looked faster and the gulls were uncertain how safe they were.

We then tried each Peregrine 'waiting-on' high over the spot where the gulls crossed. Surprisingly, this didn't frighten the gulls as much. They never flew under the falcons but they did fly near them and, it seemed that the gulls saw the falcons as lazy, in a soar, with no interest in hunting. The falcon's effectiveness to scare gulls decreased proportionally with the height gained by the falcon. The male remained effective at a greater height than the female. They were more effective when we flew the pair of falcons together, particularly when one or both falcons stooped from on high at the lure or the gulls.

The male, as I said, couldn't be induced to chase the gulls hard no matter what we tried. However, the female chased gulls and this frightened them more than anything we'd seen so far, particularly if she chased hard and failed. This seemed to signal to the gulls that she still was a danger. If she caught one, the other gulls came overhead and circled and called for about 15 minutes while she ate. They seemed to lose their fear of her. If she sat eating one of their brethren below, they could fly past in safety. If the male flew towards the gulls while they mobbed the female Peregrine, all the gulls would scatter to the nearest water and stay there for about an hour.

The gulls used four strategies to escape:

(i) they flew to any close water, even shallow water they could only stand in, and waited until the falcon disappeared or caught a gull

(ii) if they sought refuge in water from the attacking female and were forced off that water by the male falcon or a cracker shell, they circled in a tight, confusing mass

(iii) they turned their heads to face and scream at the attacking falcon just as it was about to strike

(iv) they went to the cover of vegetation if pressed hard by the attacking falcon

Gulls seemed to manage one or more types of deterrent without major confusion but, if a female falcon chased them, a cracker shell was set off, and the male falcon was used, they became confused. Moreover, when we used deterrents in this manner for two weeks, the sight of our vehicle became enough stimulus for the gulls to leave. Eventually these gulls chose another route altogether. They used a different flight path for two weeks after we stopped flying falcons on their main route. They were apparently confused and unnerved by this combination of unpredictable scare-tactics.

We had a major problem with these trials. Some flights went high and for long distances and we often lost the falcons and had to lure them in the following day or, sometimes even a week later. We lost the female in Port Lincoln just before I left and, though she was often sighted on the piers hunting pigeons around the wheat silos, we never recaptured her. I took the male Peregrine to Sydney in January 1975 to meet Tony Crosswell, one of the directors of

Longwings and later trapped a female Black Falcon and male white-morph Gray Goshawk for them to use.

From the beginning there were strong differences of opinion about how to use falcons at Sydney Airport. I thought the circumstances, species, and problems were so different in Sydney from those in Britain that the old ways would fail. These gulls flew over the runway twice a day, without landing on it as they did in England. 'Waiting-on' didn't seem to work; falcons would have to chase gulls, and catch some, and we might have to use this with multiple, carefully orchestrated deterrents. Peregrines, not Black Falcons, were the best species to use and radio-telemetry would be essential. At the time, radio-telemetry wasn't used with falcons on airports, but it was clear it would be necessary for *Longwings* at Sydney if they tried the techniques used in Port Lincoln. However, for a number of reasons, *Longwings* didn't use radio-telemetry or the techniques we tried at Port Lincoln. The personnel from *Longwings*, quite rightly, pointed to my inexperience in airport work and to their successful track record. Telemetry, they believed, was impractical and they already had experience with multiple deterrents, though, perhaps, not quite in the way I had proposed. The first time they released the male Peregrine he immediately flew away from them into Sydney and never looked back. He wasn't seen by any of us again.

At any rate I worked with *Longwings* for a month and helped where I could before leaving for Canberra. *Longwings* stayed at Sydney Airport for about 18 months but, for whatever reasons, the authorities recorded their trial as a failure. All plans for using falcons were discontinued. Some *Longwings* personnel told me, privately, that certain people strongly opposed the idea of using falcons from the beginning and chose to ignore or belittle their documented successes at Sydney Airport. They did lose many of the falcons flown there and had difficulty procuring more.

A special bird unit was formed in the Department of Civil Aviation which advised against the further use of falcons. The unit made certain that rubbish tips and other food sources were removed from near the airport and that the original program with cracker shells and shotguns continued. We'll never know if falcons could have helped at Sydney Airport.

7 Rehabilitation and Some Filming

Perth in Western Australia is bright and green in Spring 1993. I spend the evening with Katie and David who care for orphaned and injured raptors in a small rehabilitation centre on the city edge. They plan and focus all they have on this. We study, with infinite care, an injured female Peregrine that recently came to them. She's a familiar form now, stocky and strong, almost bowed legs and a proud dark eye that never is cowed. We think she'll never return to the wild because the damage is permanent.

Every year adult and juvenile raptors hit wires, cars, fences or other obstacles and the young fall from nests. People take them to use in falconry or keep as pets. Sometimes well-meaning carers make mistakes and their run of bad luck continues; the raptor dies or remains permanently captive. We hope for each hawk or falcon or eagle brought to us and lament when their freedom or life is lost.

Caring for an injured or orphaned raptor taps strong drives in us. We nurse and try desperately to return them to the sky and their own. People in rehabilitation groups all over the world devote their lives to caring for orphaned and injured wildlife. What drives us to do this? Why do we face the discomfort of forcing meat down a bird's throat only to risk a painful bereavement if it dies? People who care for raptors do feel important, they gain status and esteem from their peers. But also there seems to be, in most of us, a strong, natural drive to nurture. It may link to parenting and care of relatives. But why do we care for orphaned and injured wildlife when this caring has no evolutionary benefits for us? Would we have felt compelled to care for such animals, in prehistoric times, as companions, or curiosities, or, heaven forbid, to eat them when food was short? In the 1990's our reward is to save a life and return freedom. We protect those weaker than ourselves. This may be a more common sentiment in countries that can afford to be more caring and humanist about wildlife. Raptors are seen as our equals and we have caused, through progress, many of the injuries and deaths they face. We owe them.

Whatever the forces, our drive is strong and our failure is painful. So how do we start?

Zero

In 1970 Les Boyd brought me an old Red-tailed Hawk that veterinarians said would die. She lay, almost motionless, in the bottom of a cardboard box with her eyes closed. Apparently she'd struck a car or wire or become weak from hunger in this hard northern winter. The bitter winds in Pullman could have brought her down. To warm her I placed her in my room and cut up small pieces of beef to force down her throat. She was the first raptor I would rehabilitate.

There was a strong, almost unstoppable drive to keep her eating, make certain she lived. No real logic applied, it was emotion-driven work. Some would question, quite rightly, the ecological value of this. Why spend time with an old hawk when she may have only a few years left? Habitat destruction and extinction are the real problems we face. Why not devote our time to these more important issues? What these questions miss is the drive in us, a natural drive to help individual creatures, not just species.

Hawks this low rarely make it through their first night so Les was pleased, that next morning, when he saw her alive.

Adult male Peregrine Falcon near Canberra.

John smoking fish on Lake Lebarge.

Alan Gardner (far right) and Les Boyd (far left) hunting with a Prairie Falcon near Pullman, Washington.

Flinders Ranges and creeks near Port Augusta, South Australia.

The author trapping Peregrine Falcons near Port Augusta, South Australia.

Elizabeth, the Peregrine Falcon and Mary, the Black Falcon used in hunting and airport trials.

Peter Slater and Black Falcon at Sydney Airport.

Brown Falcon, White Goshawk, and Brown Goshawk trapped in Canberra for use in airport trials.

Yarak, the Wedge-tailed Eagle at six weeks old in Port Augusta.

Elizabeth, the Peregrine Falcon being flown to Sydney Airport for trials against Silver Gulls.

Stephen Turner with nestling White-bellied Sea Eagles near Canberra.

*The author climbing
into a Peregrine's nest
near Canberra.*

Children near Canberra releasing a rehabilitated Hobby.

Yarak and the author filming with the Leyland Brothers near Port Augusta.

Yarak catching a fox near Port Augusta.

Young Prairie Falcons, Snake River Birds of Prey Area, Idaho.

Young Peregrine Falcon near Canberra.

65

Mel Gibson being sprayed with dirt on the movie set of Mad Max III.

Les Boyd with banded Osprey on Lake Coeur d'Alene, Idaho.

Boy fishing in Bonegi Creek on Guadalcanal, Solomon Islands.

Islander preparing to take us searching for eagles in the Solomon Islands.

Young Peregrines in a pothole nest near Canberra.

Two nestling Wedge-tailed Eagles with an older captive-bred nestling from Sydney's Taronga Park Zoo.

Les Boyd with young Golden Eagle in the Snake River Birds of Prey Area, Idaho.

Elizabeth Stevenson near Canberra studying Peregrine Falcon chicks, marked blue to tell them apart.

Greenfalk studying Prairie Falcons in the Snake River Birds of Prey Area, Idaho.

70

Fledgling Australian Kestrels on hack box, near Canberra.

Prairie Falcon eyrie at Rock Lake, Washington.

Injured Collared Sparrowhawk, Canberra.

I nurtured her and, after some days, got her on her feet, got her to eat on her own and, eventually, trained and flew her in the countryside around Pullman. We called her Zero. Later that winter she flew and hunted with vehemence, as if she was grateful to be alive and able to do what she'd practiced for years. With intelligence and experience, she hunted rabbits. After she was released, we saw her for several months sitting on telephone poles some five miles from Les's house but she refused to come down to us. Finally we saw her less and less, then not at all. We hoped she moved off with a mate to raise young.

Yarak

In the spring of 1973 a Wedge-tailed eagle chick was brought to Port Augusta by kangaroo shooters who shot its parents. This rather odd phenomenon was common around Port Augusta. Shooters would kill a kangaroo or other animal then feel sorry for the orphan they created. Then they would bring the joey, or whatever kind of baby it was, and raise it or get someone else to. At any rate the man raised the baby eagle but, mistakenly, hand-fed it. The eaglet soon associated humans with food and began to scream whenever it saw humans. More alarmingly, it would walk over and try to take food from his children. After they fledge, birds of prey aggressively solicit food from their own parents, even attack them, so, when imprinted to humans, they simply do the same thing. The man asked me to take the eagle off his hands.

After the eagle's feathers were fully grown I began to train him by carefully controlling his weight then approaching him with small morsels of food. The eagle already associated people with food so the next stages came easily. He hopped to my fist, then came further and further on a long line until he was coming 30 metres.

After 10 days training, he flew free and I took him daily up Stirling Creek or to the hills near Mt Brown to fly and exercise. He followed me, like a dog follows its owner, but he flew. Though his tameness worried me, I concentrated on teaching him to hunt so he could go free. He had remarkably poor vision in dim light, which surprised us, and, unless they moved, he often couldn't see some rabbits that we could see. But, in daylight, he could see moving rabbits at much greater distances than us. His vision was remarkable and our observations were later confirmed through experimental work with another Wedge-tailed Eagle by Liz Reymond at the Australian National University in Canberra.

About this time Sterling Creek flooded and some residents couldn't reach their houses. I had a Toyota four-wheel drive and offered to take the parent of one of my students to her house across an open field covered with half a metre of water. Unfortunately, the Toyota got stuck in the middle and I had to carry her to the house on foot. When I returned to get the vehicle, I used a shovel and some planks from a nearby island poking out of the flood, to try to move the Toyota. But a man came storming through the gate, which I'd entered, and loudly and angrily accused me of disturbing graves. Apparently I had bogged the Toyota in a flooded graveyard and used the grave diggers' implements and timbers to dig out the car. As an appropriate punishment, the man locked the gate of the graveyard so I couldn't leave even if I extracted the Toyota. There was a large flooded field in front me and a locked gate behind me.

I waded home to feed the eagle knowing I'd have to wait until the Toyota was disinterred before I could fly him. The next day I returned to the graveyard where the water had drained off but the car was deeply bogged in soft mud between two graves. As I pondered the mud around me and locked gate on the cemetery road, two Jeeps appeared at the gate with *Leyland Brothers* written on their doors. The Leyland Brothers were adventurers who filmed, for television, their travels around Australia. They said they'd been looking for me because they wanted to use the eagle in their current film about flying gliders across Australia. They also offered to help disengage the Toyota from the graveyard and stretched a winch cable from their Jeeps across the muddy field to my front bumper. After fifteen minutes the Toyota was free.

The next day we filmed the eagle in flight for their gliding documentary and, because it went well, the Leylands asked if they could return in spring to make a documentary about raptors.

In October 1974 they returned to film nests of wild Peregrines, Black Falcons and Little Eagles. They filmed the Peregrines in training for the Sydney Airport trials (see Chapter 6), the rehabilitation of a Little Eagle and added this to film they originally took of the Wedge-tailed Eagle. They titled the film simply *"Birds of Prey"* and took spectacular slow-motion shots of the Little Eagle as it learned to grab prey by the head and shoulders by chasing a dead rabbit dragged on a string. Then we drove out to the red sandhills near Port Augusta where the eagle caught a rabbit and tumbled in ultra-slow motion, clutching the rabbit by the head and neck. This was one of their most successful films and one of the first to sell overseas. Mal and Mike Leyland were professional, creative film makers who weren't afraid to take chances. They were partly responsible for Australians looking away from Europe towards Australia as a tourist destination.

The Wedge-tailed Eagle progressed to the point where he flew strongly and, because I then had to train falcons for the Sydney Airport trials, I asked Terry Dennis, the ranger in Alligator Gorge Park, to finish training him, and release him there. Terry took the eagle and named him 'Yarak', an Asian word for the ultra-aggressive and rather dangerous state that trained eagles and accipiters come into when they're hungry. Terry worked hard to care for the environment and his work with the eagle was exemplary. He was patient, methodical, and grew to understand the bird much better than anyone. Yarak emerged as a hunter under Terry's guidance. As I was preparing this book, he wrote to me about two memorable flights:

" After about six weeks of getting to know each other and the hard work of daily training flights, Yarak took very quickly to just following me overhead when I went off trekking around the ranges near my home. He was so imprinted and, after all, I was the provider.

He would come strongly to the lure, so there was never any real thought of him wandering off. I got him following the old Land Rover as well. I had to really, as there were few rabbits back in the ranges and this bird had to learn to find its own way in the world. Actually it was quite easy.

I got bored with the training routine and so did Yarak, my mad dashes across the flat doing the 'dead rabbit on a string' trick just got too easy no matter how I tried to trick him. I would only get 30 yards and he had it nailed! So, I simply increased the length of the cord and hung onto it out of the window of the Land Rover ...... It wasn't long and even my best erratics with the string couldn't fool him.

After that, once released he would sit in his favourite perching tree and scream at me every time I showed until the games began! Then he shut up and got very serious.

One day I was called out to some situation in the Park, forgetting that Yarak was free and waiting for me, I drove off several miles with Yarak and I arriving at the same time. The people were most impressed!

After that I could drive out of the ranges to where the rabbits were thick, often up to 30 miles or so, out onto the Willochra Plains, with no problems unless there were other eagles around. He made a lot of mistakes, but it wasn't long and he got very good at nailing those bunnies! I was still 'calling' him off the kills to the glove, which was OK for a while but he started getting very possessive and some days, **very** mad at me! Mantling over the kill and like daring me to do my disappearing trick with **his** food!

One day we were out on the plain with rabbits going everywhere when Yarak stooped fast and low out of sight amongst low lignum bushes about 50 yards off. When I got there I found him on a half grown ginger feral cat! The cat was very dead and Yarak busy ripping fur off.....

Soon after this we were out in the foothills above Wilmington one day, with me walking along a lightly timbered razor-back ridge and Yarak circling 'waiting on' overhead, very hungry and very fit. At that time we were a team I guess; he was waiting for me to flush a rabbit. We had been at this quite a bit now and we both knew what the other was doing most of the time. Then, before I knew it, he was off in a tightly folded stoop very fast off to my left and down below the line of the ridge and out of sight.

That's a bit strange, I was thinking, as I raced over to where the ridge dropped away sharply below an escarpment, but nothing in what the bird had done previously prepared me for the sight of Yarak tumbling downslope, wings out trying to gain some control and dignity, firmly footed onto the neck of an almost full grown fox!

I ran ... stumbled down the fifty yards or so, thinking as I went, you dumb bird ... just when it looked as if you might make it you go and get yourself chewed up by an animal that weighed three or four times your weight, and with teeth! As I arrived Yarak was on the fox and they were both sort of upright with the fox looking a bit shaky and Yarak very mad! Every feather standing on end. Quick! a decision, what to do? I moved in close and shot the fox, end of contest. I had never seen Yarak so worked up, (me too!). It took me ten minutes to calm down and several attempts to get the bird off. Ghengis Khan hunted wolves using Golden Eagles from horse back ... didn't he ...?

A mistake? Maybe, but that eagle was wild from that time on......"

When Peter Slater and I took falcons to Sydney Airport for the first trial (see Chapter 6 above), we were met by a film maker, Vic Martin, who filmed the first and second trial and asked if he could come to Port Augusta that winter, to film the falcons and Yarak in training. We agreed that Vic would come and spend most of his time following Terry and Yarak around the hills near Port Augusta and Alligator Gorge. Vic worked very hard and always considered the needs of the birds. It was a pleasure to work with such a professional. The film was eventually shown on television as "*A Search for the Eagle*".

Flying birds for the camera is hard. Even large species, like Wedge-tailed Eagles, are difficult to follow, so the trainer must communicate to the man or woman holding the camera precisely what the bird will do and then make certain the bird does it. Terry did this admirably and organized many good shots for the film including one illustrating an eagle's long-range vision. He called Yarak from nearly a kilometre away, further away than humans could see him, and the eagle flew from a speck on the horizon, right up to the camera, all filmed in slow motion.

With filming completed, and warmer weather coming, Terry released Yarak in Alligator Gorge National Park. He was seen once or twice after that but then disappeared. We always worried about Yarak's tameness and wondered if he got in trouble. I doubt we'll ever know.

Readymix

Readymix was an injured Peregrine Falcon found by the side of a road near Canberra some five kilometres from the nest where she fledged. I'd banded her as a nestling in November 1984, three months before, in an abandoned Readymix cement quarry - hence the name. She was thin and weak lying on the floor of the cage and couldn't hold her injured wing off the ground. No broken bones were apparent but the shoulder joint was strained or broken so it would be some time before she could go. Most birds of prey don't need to be flown to be rehabilitated but she was flown to determine the extent of damage to her shoulder. While being rehabilitated, she would appear in three documentaries - *Earthwatch: Birds of Prey*, *Hunters of the Skies*, and *Under Control*.

After Readymix's weight doubled, and she was out of danger, her training started. At first she was reluctant to take food from my fingers or eat in my presence. But she was fed at the same time each day and, because I repeatedly approached her with small bits of meat, she grew tamer. The way you approach a wild raptor is crucial to building trust. You don't approach directly, you come in from an angle, obliquely, and keep low and slow. You don't look directly at her, you look to the side and watch her out the corner of your eye. Direct stares can signal threat of attack to raptors.

We decided early to tame her only enough to fly her. After all, she was to be released, freed, and even though she appeared in some films on the way, she'd retain some wildness, some mistrust of humans.

So, after a week of approaching her with food, earning her trust and equating my visits with food, I tried to get her to step onto my gloved fist and feed there. When I placed my gloved fist holding a piece of meat low and in front of her, just out of reach, she reached, craned her neck trying hard to get the meat without stepping onto my fist. Eventually she stepped slowly and carefully onto the glove, reached down to the meat held in her yellow toes, tore a piece off and swallowed. But she kept looking up at me with one dark eye before reaching down to pull another piece.

Training a falcon for release should progress every day. The falcon should do something new even though she tries to get you to give her meat for doing yesterday's task, or even less. The next day I tried to get her to feed on the fist while I walked. Slowly, hesitantly and with some mistrust, she ate while we walked. Walking through countryside, a serene time to think, you talk to the falcon, accustom her to your voice, and develop trust. She looks over at you, rocks on your glove, sometimes clutching her talons through it, sometimes sticking out one brown wing then the other. Her sweet breath is clean when she's close to your face. A falcon's breath is always sweet, surprising given the foul stench of other predators like dogs and some humans. Over the next few days I walked with her and talked to her, stopping to set her on fence posts or grey eucalypt limbs. From there I called her off the posts to meat on the glove. She had a long line attached to the jesses on her legs, the distances increased day by day until she came 30 metres. Then she was taught to come to a lure, a leather bag swung through the air, that was later used to exercise her. She learned to chase the lure in the air, and, when she caught it, was rewarded with food.

Readymix could now fly free, with no lines or encumbrances. This is a nervous moment but, with experience, one learns to gauge the right time, understand when a falcon has progressed far enough to take this first free flight and return. I released her, she flew in a wide arc out, circled around, and came back to the lure. After that she was left outdoors alone for a few hours each day to fly and build muscle and endurance, then brought back in for the night.

The A.B.C.'s *Earthwatch* filmed some of this rehabilitation process with Readymix. Filming is a very slow process with a lot of waiting around. If the cameraman missed a shot, she had to do repeated performances and, sometimes, if we left her out for hours while we organized cameras and discussed shots, she grew impatient. At one point, in a rage, she jumped off the fist into my face and cut me just below the eye. Another time she flew over the crew and killed a young Magpie in heavy brush. They rushed in to film her but it all happened too fast and she cackled at them and flew off. More about Readymix in Chapter 8.

The *Earthwatch* director, David Telfer, was far less dogmatic than other film makers I'd worked with. At one point I asked if he'd include two girls from the local Barnardo's home. They had been suspended from school and I was trying to get them back in. They could be helped by this opportunity. The girls agreed and David agreed so they, the girls, brought in an injured Peregrine for me to examine and the scene was included in the final film.

The A.B.C. crew were excellent to work with. Their working conditions were far superior to the conditions of documentary makers from the private sector. They were fatter too.

Orlik

Orlik, a male Wedge-tailed Eagle, was found starving at
the Queanbeyan rubbish tip near Canberra. He was tame,
obviously hand-raised, and brought to us by the New South
Wales National Parks and Wildlife Service. I eventually
passed him to Robert Bartos, a Czech national, who left
Czechoslovakia in 1968 after the Russians invaded and stole
his parent's jewellery and other possessions. As he and some
friends stood across a road blocking a tank, a Russian soldier got out of the tank, aimed a rifle at Robert's friend standing next to him and killed him with a shot to the head. In
1968 Robert swam across a river from Czechoslovakia after
he and a soldier friend got drunk. His friend agreed to look
the other way, Robert wasn't shot at, and he made it to Aus-
tria, Germany and, eventually, New Guinea and Australia.
A warrant was issued for his arrest if he returned. Robert
was and is a particularly charitable and generous man, but,
understandably, he hates Russians. Twenty years later,
working as a chef in Canberra, the Russian basketball team
came in to the restaurant and Robert dropped everything
and walked out.

'Orlik' is Czechoslovakian for eagle. While in Czechoslovakia, Robert handled and trained many hawks and eagles.
He flew, for some time, an Imperial Eagle for audiences at
the Prague Zoo until this eagle attacked a girl in a fur jacket
and actually held the child down until Robert came to lift it
off. Robert is also a gifted inventor and artist, who later
would design and build a new raptor trap, and illustrate
the rehabilitation book *'Caring for Birds of Prey'*. By the
time Orlik came to us, both Robert and I knew the dangers
of flying eagles.

Robert began to train Orlik and soon had him flying free.
But Orlik never seemed to fly strongly. Apparently he'd been
under-nourished by those who raised him. Many raptors
are underfed in captivity because people don't realise how
much they need to maintain their body weight and grow.
And, if they aren't flown during the crucial developmental
stage after they fledge, eagles and falcons never develop

ample flying skills to hunt and survive. That is, an eagle or falcon that is caged for its first year can usually be flown free and may look strong to the untrained eye. But, no matter how much it's flown, it will never have the strength and co-ordination to hunt properly because it didn't fly, develop co-ordination and endurance during those crucial months after its feathers were grown. This was the case with Orlik; he'd be with us for good.

As it happened, Orlik appeared on television in four wildlife documentaries, one jeans advertisement, and one feature film. This was largely because Robert taught him in such an innovative manner. He trained Orlik to leave a perch, usually a tree branch, and fly in a wide circle then back to the tree branch. This proved particularly helpful to cameramen who needed a predictable target for their narrow-scope, telephoto lenses. Robert and Orlik gave them this control and predicability. Wildlife documentary makers could mix shots of Orlik with shots of nesting, soaring and hunting wild eagles to fill in the gaps and give a clearer story line to their films. The A.B.C.'s Earthwatch crew shot superb slow-motion shots of Orlik flying across a field to a fence post, small feathers lifting on the upper surfaces of his great wings. Orlik, unlike Readymix, was patient and tame and would walk around between members of the film crew like a big turkey while they prepared shots. Most of the time he was around people, he gave a light plaintive whistle, a very gentle tone that most wouldn't connect with an eagle.

Orlik became a working eagle, generating funds for our field research and raptor rehabilitation. He visited dozens of schools to help us teach children about raptors and conservation and he was even inducted as the official mascot of Evatt Primary School in Canberra.

Orlik did one television ad, for Amco jeans. Eagles have long been admired for their great strength, keen eyesight and enviable powers of flight. Their image has often been used by strategists as a symbol of real or imagined power. The ancient Romans, various German empires, Poland, Spain and Mexico are among the many who have a symbolic eagle on their coat of arms. Barclay's, and countless other companies, proudly display eagle emblems to the world, signifying power and security. Eagles still represent military prowess, as they have for centuries; "Corporal Courage", Wedge-tailed Eagle mascot of the Australian Army's Second Cavalry Regiment, is carried as a symbol of the regiment's reconnaissance role.

Advertisers are well aware of the impact of eagles. So Robert and I found ourselves, one foggy, grey morning, arriving at a film location with Orlik. Two solid days of filming was later cut down to one thirty-second, $120,000 jeans commercial. Orlik did his trick perfectly, flying from his perch out in a circle and back so the camera crew got clear aerial shots. They were disappointed on the first day because Orlik could barely fly. He'd been moulting, hadn't been flown and was unfit. But, by the second day he was flying more strongly and even dipping down having an aerial swipe at the camera crew. Another day in the studio and we were finished. Orlik charged a reasonable $500.00 per day.

We asked director Ian Fowler why so much time and energy went into filming Orlik. He replied that the AMCO trademark was an eagle, a powerful symbol of dominance. The association between an unshackled, flying eagle and freedom was simple and effective.

The finished television ad successfully equated a jeans-wearing lifestyle with freedom. An independent young man pulled on his jeans and escaped the city down a dirt road in his yellow Ford convertible (we watched them shoot the scene no less than ten times then carefully clean the convertible after each take). Juxtaposed with these images were those of an eagle bursting from a "cage" (the studio shots) to fly free. On the soundtrack a rock group sings: "Born to fly, born to get away like an eagle. I was born to fly".

Sadly, after Robert moved to coastal New South Wales, Orlik was cornered on his perch by a giant, marauding Goanna and killed. Robert's family mourned him for some time and may still.

8 At the Movies

Down the Wind and Lost Weekend

On four occasions I was asked to use falcons or eagles on feature films. The first, in 1975, was a small-budget film called *Down the Wind*, shot in Adelaide by Kim Mackenzie, who now makes films for the Institute for Aboriginal Studies in Canberra, and Scott Hicks, from Adelaide. The film starred Penny Hackforth Jones and David Cameron, and used a Peregrine in several scenes, the falcon later given to *Longwings Incorporated* at Sydney Airport. A second film in 1977 called *Lost Weekend*, filmed near Bega, New South Wales, starred John Hargreaves and Briony Behets. It used a number of animals, including raptors, in a story rather like Hitchcock's *Birds* where animals turn on a couple who eventually meet their demise trapped in the bush.

On *Down the Wind* we tried a number of times to get shots of the Peregrine in flight but he was just too fast. In the end we settled for a shot of him feeding on a Galah in a gorge and looking down on the lead actor David Cameron. This, and the documentaries with Leylands and Vic Martin, prepared us for the difficulties that cameramen have with falcons in flight. In later films we would learn how to make these zippy fliers, who could cross the sky in seconds, more predictable through the viewfinder.

These films also prepared us for the waiting around, and the occasional bad tempers that flared from waiting and repeating the same scene over and over, until the director finds it acceptable. I had trouble getting the Brown Goshawk, Felice, to do what the director wanted and he grew angry and cold and finally refused to speak to me. During another wait, John Hargreaves blew up and stormed off the set, an empty road on a very cold morning where John's character was supposed to be killed by a semi-trailer truck. After running in front of the oncoming truck some six times and lying on the wet road for over half an hour John, quite understandably, had enough and blew. But he was professional and returned in five minutes to finish the scene which culminated in the truck smashing into a very lifelike replica of John's head.

Ground Zero

Ground Zero is a film starring Jack Thomson, Donald Pleasance, Burnam Burnam and Colin Friels. A political thriller, the story begins with the premise that above-ground nuclear tests conducted at Maralinga by the British in the 1950's could have irradiated Aboriginals living there. In his efforts to uncover the British and Australian government cover-up, Colin Friels travels to the site of the bomb test (really Coober Pedy) and meets a blind Donald Pleasance living in an elaborately decorated cave. The director, Michael Patterson, wanted a falcon to fly into the camp where Pleasance lived and carry off a mouse. Readymix wouldn't be good at this because Peregrines lack manoeuvrability and she wasn't tame so Robert Bartos kindly allowed me to use Ebony, the injured male Black Falcon he trained and was rehabilitating.

We flew to Adelaide from Canberra but they wouldn't allow the falcon on the bus or the small airlines from Adelaide to Coober Pedy so I rented a car and drove through the night. Coober Pedy is a frontier town that exists for opal mining. The town can shock the uninitiated. There are some rough standing buildings but most of the town is underground in renovated mine tunnels, under a flat, treeless 'gibber' plain

covered with hundreds of dirt piles. Each pile has an abandoned mine shaft next to it and, though some are made safe,
most are dangerous pits that can swallow a car and have
swallowed people.

The producer rented an underground room for Ebony and
me with the standard trickle of water in the shower. All
water is trucked into Coober Pedy except for that caught
from people's rooves and stored in tanks near their houses.
We were to be on the set at 6 A.M. the following morning.

The site, bare hills and caves, was filled with trucks, technicians, actors, directors and many people whose role was
never clear. We worked through the morning taking about
ten sequences of Ebony catching and carrying off a mouse
from Donald Pleasance's camp, and a scene with the falcon
perched, in close-up, with the camp below him. Ebony returned after each take.

Donald Pleasance was an English gentleman, unassuming,
professional and friendly. Given the strange roles he had
played over the years, I wasn't sure what to expect. But he
talked little of himself, listened politely to the stories of
others, and showed no sense of the prima donna. Conditions were rough in Coober Pedy but he gave no indication
that they were any less comfortable than a fine house in
the English countryside.

The quiet manner and eloquence of Burnam Burnam, the
Aboriginal activist and actor, gained the solid respect of
everyone on the set. One morning the make-up woman inadvertently scraped sand into Burnam's eye and, in an effort to remove it, badly scratched his cornea. Burnam was
stoic and quiet through the whole incident and didn't com-
plain after.

It was intriguing to see how focussed and goal-oriented the
crews were on *Ground Zero* and other film sets. There were
shows of bad temper but, on all film sets, there was a sense
of hurried, group cohesion towards a common goal that one
seldom sees in schools, universities and other institutions.

For teams and organisations aiming to conserve and rehabilitate wildlife, there is something to learn about this pin-
point focus, the clear marshalling of resources towards distinct common goals.

These film makers use raptors for good reason, their power
and attractiveness to the public. We also need to better understand, as do the *Peregrine Fund* in North America, the
power of a falcon or eagle's image in print or film as a force
that can save species.

Mad Max III: Beyond Thunderdome

In 1986 I was telephoned by *Kennedy / Miller Films* who were
working on *Mad Max III: Beyond Thunderdome*. George
Miller, the director, had a memory from childhood, or perhaps a dream, of a falcon sailing in while he and his friends
were flying a paper kite. The falcon caught the kite in the
air as the kids watched from below. He wanted a falcon to
do this for a group of children flying a kite in *Beyond
Thunderdome*. By then Readymix had experience on three
documentaries and was reliable for film work, but she wasn't
tame so I always distanced her from people.

To train her for the film, I started feeding her on the kite
made up by the *Kennedy-Miller* props department. After she
grew accustomed to this, my children, Peter and Anna, flew
the kite, first low to the ground, then higher and higher.
Food was tied to the centre of the back of the kite and, each
time, Readymix would grab the kite where the sticks crossed
at the back, descend with the kite to the field below her,
and feed. After three weeks, her performance was flawless.
She was ready to travel to the film set. However, the
Kennedy-Miller people phoned and said they'd shot far too
much film and couldn't fit the scene in. I asked if they wanted
to see Readymix catch the kite but they said no. They did,
however, want her brought down, with Orlik Wedge-tailed
Eagle, to be filmed in the children's camp.

Though it was disappointing that George Miller, the director of *Mad Max III*, didn't want Readymix or Orlik the ea-

gle flown on the set, it was heartening that he wanted them in shots of the children's camp. The story involved a clan of children, survivors of a jet crash that killed all their parents, who developed a society, language and religion based on the downed jetliner. Mad Max, Mel Gibson, comes to the camp and helps them. They shot some of the film in Coober Pedy, in South Australia, on the barren plains there, and part in Blackheath, in the Blue Mountains of New South Wales. I arrived there late at night in bitter cold and found the film company had taken over much of the town. Their headquarters in an old dishevelled multi-story centre was not unlike a set from *Mad Max II*. Many of the workers there were grimy and looked more like workers on an oil rig than workers on a very expensive movie. Everyone, though, was kind. They found a room for Readymix, Orlik and me and asked us to present in the gorge at 6 A.M. for shooting.

In the morning, I travelled down the narrow road to the "children's camp" where an army of technicians, trucks, extras, caterers, camera crew, and all the specialists used in a big film, crowded onto the set. They had constructed a completely life-like cliff at one side of the camp, and several huts on stilts between the giant eucalypts. Each of these huts was completely fitted inside with cooking implements, fires, bedding, all like a realistic camp so they could shoot interior and exterior shots. Smoking wasn't allowed on the set but we breathed smoke all day anyway. To give a misty atmosphere to the camp, technicians burned sharp-smelling baby oil in small canisters, 'smokers' as they called them.

After two hours, an assistant introduced me to the director, George Miller, who discussed, with me, the shots he wanted. The eagle and falcon would only be perched in the children's' camp to add to the cluttered, rich atmosphere they tried to create there. Because these would be close-ups with some children, the child actors would have to acquaint themselves with both birds. Because she was to be released after filming, Readymix was quite wild. We perched her high on the scaffolding of one of the children's huts and left her there. Orlik perched lower, near the children for some close-up shots. He was accustomed to children because of all his work

in schools, but he occasionally reached out to bite and, because there were so many small children on the set, I had to
watch him carefully. I held Orlik on the fist, took him in
and tied him to the railing of a hut with children next to
him for each shot, then picked him up again after each take.
George Miller was warm, personable and intense. He trained
as a medical doctor which explains the realistic gore he was
able to put into the *Mad Max* films. He was particularly
diplomatic with people. There was a dispute because some
locals wanted to use the gorge and felt these outsiders had
no right to alter the landscape and ban locals from the set.
Kennedy-Miller had to protect their stars and the film's plot
from the public and allowed no outsiders to visit the set and
no-one but the official photographers could have cameras
(they kindly made me an exception). These locals were probably right but Miller gently persuaded them, looking like a
smiling, benign Buddha, that it had to be this way and they
would have their park back in a few days. There was a vague-
ness about the way he planned scenes, he seemed a dreamer
and not a details man. It seemed like he told his dreams to
his lieutenants and they and the technicians made the
dreams happen. I wondered after the film came out if the
character who fights Mel Gibson in the Thunderdome, the
dwarf who rides atop a great, stupid being and directs this
being to do the actual fighting, was George Miller directing
his crew.

Readymix was tied to the top of a hut on scaffolding. She
stayed during the filming of a sequence where Mel Gibson
wakes in the hut, tethered by a rope around his ankle, and
rolls out backwards to fall into water below. The scene was
shot over and over until they got it right. The head animal
wrangler for the film, the person responsible for organising
animals for various shots, introduced me to Mel Gibson.
Each morning he had to be made up and this included dirt
and rubber. They sprayed him, Helen Buday and other actors, with dirt each morning and this obviously annoyed
him as he picked at dirt and bits of rubber on his face, but
he said nothing about it. When talking to him his voice had
a tendency towards cracking, almost breaking, that gave
him particular power on film. He was nervous and, at first,

seemed like a cluster of barely controlled energies. He screwed up his face and detonated into laughter. But, when he channelled this nervousness into acting, the energies projected as force. He was particularly interested in the eagle and we talked for some time about Orlik before I had to do the next take. He appeared to see himself as ordinary and was determined to ignore the fuss. The children on the set were particularly fond of him and he was skilled with them and conveyed that he liked them. He also seemed more interested in mixing with technicians and crew rather than writers and directors but he spent much of his time alone and tended to ignore people or look through them. He was surprisingly frank and told me that he was burnt-out from making too many films in too short a time but the money was simply too good to stop. He needed a rest and planned to have it after this film. He said he considered himself American, as he was born there, even though his family lived in Australia. The animal wranglers particularly liked him because he never complained about working with any animal. They put spiders, monkeys, all sorts of animals on him for various shots and he just did the shot without complaining. He clowned around a lot. We watched rushes each night and, at the end of many shots, Gibson would make a face or do something silly to break the tension.

After this film, when Readymix turned three, she was released near Canberra in the area where she'd done much of her training and filming. She stayed for about two weeks, then drifted off as spring came. We thought we saw her, one year, defending young at a local eyrie.

9 The Solomon Islands

We met Teu Zingihite some three hours earlier and knew very little about him. Now we huddled under a plastic sheet in his narrow dugout canoe far from any visible land in the storm-tossed sea. The rain and wind slapped and pushed us as we cowered, most un-intrepid, and discussed, yelling into each other's ears (the storm was so loud he never would have heard us), whether we should have trusted this man who said he could take us, safely, from Gizo, in the Western Provinces of the Solomon Islands, to the island of Kolombangara. Experienced men disappeared each year in these dugouts when storms caught them at sea and they drowned or were eaten by sharks. The smaller dugouts were notoriously unstable and the Japanese, when they invaded the Solomon Islands in 1942, had to tie three or four together to prevent them capsizing. My colleague, Sue, an experienced sailor, assured me that Teu must know what he was doing because of the way he used the prow to cut through the two-metre-high waves.

Teu yelled at us, dripping in the back of the dugout, and we looked back at him. He pointed to the horizon - "My village", he said, and we could see a line of coconut palms two kilometres away and some wispy smoke, but the storm stung our faces so we hunkered back down under the plastic. Hopefully, in the storm, he could navigate the last part of the journey across this stretch of open ocean and into the narrow break in the coral reef that protected his village from the sea.

The Solomon Islands is a new nation, a scattered double chain of 992 islands, atolls and cays in the south-west Pacific. These islands vary from the largest, Guadalcanal, about 160 kilometres long and 48 kilometres wide with mountains and cloud forest 2440 metres high, to tiny low-lying coral atolls. Most islands are covered by dense rain-forest, and rainfall can be four metres a year. The Solomons, which lie near the equator just west of Papua New Guinea, north-east of Australia and north-west of Fiji, were given their independence from Britain in 1978. The islands are full of small subsistence villages where mainly Melanesian families survive from fishing and small gardens near their thatched huts. Population pressures could change all that.

Everyone we met spoke three languages - pidgin, their local dialect and some English. English could often be the weakest of the three and children would practice theirs on us, yelling "Hello" and "I am Harry" as we walked through the streets.

In September 1990 we visited the Solomons to look for the Solomon Islands Sea Eagle, also known as Sanford's Eagle, to determine whether it still existed and how hard it would be to study. The International Council for Bird Preservation listed it, along with the Pied Sparrowhawk, another endemic Solomon Islands species, as endangered. Our objectives were to find the eagle, photograph it if possible as we knew of no existing photographs, locate a nest of the eagle, and find out from locals how rare it was. We also hoped to see the Pied Goshawk, Solomon Islands Boobook Owl and Fearful Owl as almost nothing was known of their ecology.

As you fly over the high mountains into Honiara on Guadalcanal, the beauty of the place stuns you. There are waterfalls in deep gullies, cloud forests on high verdant mountain flanks surrounded by warm, blue seas. But many are shocked when they land and disembark in Honiara. The streets are poor and dirty and the black population eyes with suspicion, and perhaps some contempt, the white tourists. There is good reason for this in the history of these islands. Their people were taken as slaves to work in the cane fields of Queensland and Fiji at the end of the 19th century, their villages have been shelled by Australian gunboats, and they were forcefully governed by the British for decades. After the Japanese invaded during World War II, the islanders hid from them and generally sided with the Allies. These islanders witnessed one of the great land and sea battles in history where dozens of ships sank into Ironbottom Sound in a great American defeat, and a small group of U.S. Marines held the land around Henderson field on Guadalcanal for an American victory. Historians say it was the turning point in the Pacific war. Some Japanese soldiers hid there in the jungle for twenty years, before emerging, and we saw many Japanese tourists visiting the battlefields and graves. Some took home, in small wooden boxes, bones and fragments, and identification tags they believed were from relatives.

Catholic and Seventh-Day Adventist churches predominate in the Solomons, and only recently replaced a belief system that included head hunting. Strong tribes would raid weaker tribes, steal their women and murder the men. For good luck they mounted the severed heads of their enemies on the front of the victors' canoes. Head hunting was curtailed by Christianity but also by force. British administrators warned in the 1930's that head hunting must stop. The next group of men caught beheading their neighbours were quickly and publicly hung. The practice died out but stone and wooden heads are available for sale all over the Solomons and given as gifts. Still there is a feeling of subterranean violence there. This may seem unrelated to ornithology but we found it was crucial to understand some of this past and society to avoid offending and gain help from the locals. It is impossible to study raptors in the Solomons without this help.

So entering Honiara was like entering an impoverished third world country where the locals glare at 'Europeans' in bitterness. The next day, we left for islands in the Western Provinces starting with Gizo the capital. There we would start our search for the Solomon Sea Eagle.

After climbing into a Solomon Islands Air Service plane we were immediately reassured by the faith of the pilot. Before taking off, he turned around in his seat and asked us all to pray with him. We hadn't prayed for quite some time, longer than we could remember, but this man obviously knew more about flying in the Solomon Islands than we did, so we bowed our heads, closed our eyes and repeated after him - "Dear father, please ensure a safe trip for us all and watch over us. Amen." Then we lifted out of Honiara to fly some 450 kilometres over hundreds of islands and atolls, some covered with coconut plantations and others carpeted with vibrant, green rainforest.

As we approached the village of Gizo, on the island of Ghizo, we could see a slim grassy strip on a tiny offshore island. The island of Ghizo is about 11 kilometres long with no flat spots for an airstrip. We saw no way he could land on this cricket pitch from that high up but, perhaps owing to his prayers, we bounced safely down the grass strip and stopped. We then helped to unload the luggage into a long boat docked near the strip. This motored across a narrow strait to Gizo where we booked into the Gizo Hotel.

There was only one 'international standard' hotel in the Solomon Islands, that is, one where you could get a room with air conditioning, but it was a long way from Gizo. We were near the equator, had just come from snow in the Canberra winter and hoped for more than a room fan. But a room fan would do.

Our plan was to look for raptors in some of the remnant forest on Ghizo so we asked locals about transport. Could we rent a car, a motorbike, a push bike or taxi? People looked at us strangely until, after a morning of asking dozens of people, we finally got the message. The way out of town was on foot. We found an Osprey nest on our first walk but the forest was thick and very hot. We bought umbrellas to shield us from the sun, and, though it was the 'dry season', to keep out of the daily afternoon bucketing, rain you can only know if you've been in the tropics. After two days of frustration trying to get out of Gizo, I finally went down to the main street to rent a bike from a local. The first boy I asked said yes, for an exorbitant $20, and I was free. People laughed at this strange middle-aged white man cycling down dirt roads on a child's bicycle that kept losing its chain, but it was a way out of town. I saw a Pied Goshawk and Ospreys on the bike trips but no eagles.

We decided to find a way to Kolombangara, a large island some 20 kilometres east of Ghizo, that we could see each morning before clouds covered its volcanic summit. Kolombangara, sometimes called Nduke by residents, had been logged and there was remnant forest around the tops of Mounts Veve and Tapalamenggutu, two volcanic cones towards the centre of the island. This may seem like an odd place to look for sea eagles but searching for raptors in these islands was quite different from searching in America or the Australian bush. There was almost no transport in the islands and little visibility once you were down in the rainforest. Reports we had from locals claimed the eagle nested on mountain slopes, not on the ocean shore. We had failed, so far, to see an eagle and would be better off looking in patches of jungle instead of huge swathes of impenetrable, continuous forest.

We asked around town and two people told us of Teu Zingihite, who lived on Kolombangara and had worked with the eminent ornithologist and writer Jared Diamond from the University of California at Los Angeles. We met him at the Gizo markets where he came weekly to sell vegetables from his village garden. Teu, short, with some greying at the temples, and in his early 50's, was warm and gregarious. We had lunch in Gizo and talked about the eagle. He knew of nests as a boy, and remembered one he found while dodging the Japanese on Kolombangara. But he hadn't seen a nest for some years.

The eagle, with the saltwater crocodile, shark and snake, were totems in the old religion. They were worshipped and never killed. But, with the advent of Christianity, eagles became vermin, threats to the poultry introduced by Catholic missionaries and others. So, they were shot, became wary and no longer nested near villages. I could find no descriptions in the literature of a nest.

We loaded ourselves into Teu's narrow dugout canoe for the trip across to Kolombangara. He reassured us that we'd be fine when, suddenly, midway across, a storm hit. Teu stayed out, squinting into the storm, navigating with his small outboard motor while we sheltered under plastic and one umbrella and hoped the giant waves didn't flip us into the sea. This was within a few kilometres of Plum Pudding Island, where John F. Kennedy's PT-109 went down, but we'd feel no glamour if we capsized and had to swim, in this storm, to the same island.

As we reached the island, Teu navigated through a narrow channel in the coral reef that surrounded most of Kolombangara and protected his village. The village looked like paradise with a pure white beach, palm trees backed by rainforest, and further back, the 1770 metre peaks of the extinct volcano, Mount Veve.

The village had no running water, no showers or baths, no toilets and none of the twenty or so huts had any glass windows. There were no roads, people walked or boated. Villagers used the local mangroves as toilets, which twice a day were flushed by the tide, and they used various clear jungle pools every day to bath. Villagers caught some fish but also used tinned fish from a Western Provinces tuna cannery and grew vegetables and some chocolate. The main cash crop was copra from the local coconut palms. Life was clean and orderly in Teu's village.

Teu's wife, Mary, led us up stairs into their house made from poles and palm fronds on ten-foot-high stilts. After we washed in a jungle pool and slept in Teu's house for an hour, he took us up to explore a small river that ran from Mount

Veve, near the centre of the island, down to the sea near his village. He had seen eagles near there and thought they may nest up the hill along the river. We'd been in the Solomon Islands for nearly a week with no sign of an eagle, though we'd seen many Ospreys and Brahminy Kites. We worked our way up through the cocoa plantation and market garden then into the forest along the river. Teu hacked through the close vegetation with his machete. At one point he looked at the sky and dashed to cut giant fronds from a low tree. "Put these over you. Quickly!" he said. Within 30 seconds a tropical storm poured down. Ten minutes later the rain stopped, we left the fronds on the ground and followed Teu up the hill.

There were nests of an Osprey, Brahminy Kite and Varied Goshawk but no eagles. We watched the goshawk nest for two hours. The same species breeds on the east coast of Australia but is a large white or grey hawk that kills rabbits and forest pigeons. This Solomon Islands form was rufous and grey, though its single young was grey and white, as with the Australian type. The Solomon Islands form was only the size of a sparrowhawk, about 150 to 200 grams, whereas the Australian form is four times this size. This pair caught small brown skinks, and Holland, the land owner, told me it also caught his baby chickens. This made him less than happy and he threatened to cut down the tree. We returned to Teu's village with no prospect of seeing an eagle. Sadly, some villagers told us that the Catholic brothers at nearby Vanga Point had shot the local eagles because they attacked ducks, chickens, cats and dogs. The eagle, it seems, had been much safer as a religious totem when Solomon Islanders hunted each other than it was under Christian theology.

We learned, that night, how noisy tropical villages can be. A Barn Owl nested outside the window and fed its single young through the night. The young have a particularly rasping and piercing call that screeched into our room from dusk until dawn. We probably should have watched more carefully but we didn't realise that a Barn Owl's nest hadn't been described for the Solomon Islands. Many other night animals called from the jungle, dogs barked and, soon after, roosters crowed.

Two more days searching found us no eagles, only frustration. Teu took us up another river to show us an old nest near the top of a giant rainforest tree, a giant dilapidated nest much like the nest of the White-bellied Sea Eagle.

On the third day, Saturday, Teu told us the village, all Seventh-Day Adventists, would spend the day at the pole-and-fronds church on the shore. Teu warned me not to venture into the jungle alone. It was dangerous and I needed local knowledge to stay out of trouble. But, after reading for two hours, I wanted out so decided to ignore his advice and walked to the nearby river, driven to find an eagle. I waded into the water and up as far as was passable to look for them in the forest. There were Brahminy Kites there - strange, as they normally are strictly coastal, but here they flew around under the forest canopy like Red-shouldered Hawks. Varied Goshawks were common in the forest and there was a pair in the first 100 metres and another pair 200 metres further. As I walked in off the river towards this second pair to observe them more closely, my skin suddenly began to burn and welt like it had touched nettles. It worsened and, by the time the source of the burning was clear, I was trapped. It was a small bushy tree and I'd have to force my way back 50 metres through these same trees to reach the safety of the river. Carefully I picked up a stick from the forest floor and, pushing each branch aside, worked under, over and around the trees for 20 minutes to go the thirty metres back to the river.

Teu only laughed when I returned, offering no consolation and repeated the story about the stupid 'European' to his friends and family. I couldn't sleep that night and very little the next until the red welts started to disappear.

We decided to travel in Teu's canoe to Ringgi on the southeast side of Kolombangara. This former logging settlement had a few European-style houses and a new forestry development. *Kolombangara Forest Products* were planting tree seedlings from New Guinea, a similar species to the one Teu's canoe was carved from, but faster growing. The Solomon Islands have very few roads so we thought we could more easily gain access to the higher interior of the island from the old logging roads near Ringgi. This could be where we would find eagles. Ringgi was the only place on the island where there were vehicles. Teu and Mary visited their son, who worked in the logging industry in Ringgi, then left for their village.

Tony Fraser, and the other forestry managers at Ringgi, were very kind. They organized accommodation and drove us each day up the flanks of Mount Reno to leave us in the rainforest. Ringgi had a dated colonial atmosphere, with Europeans living high on the hill in spacious houses with well-kept gardens and the Melanesian workers down the hill in small iron or wood huts. Again there was an atmosphere of simmering anger against some whites and some Malaitans. There was a weekly ferry service from Gizo to Ringgi and back to Honiara. But, the week before we arrived, there had been a fight on board between Malaitans and locals with fighters crawling up over the captain's cabin and all over the boat, trying to get at each other. The captain now refused to stop at Ringgi so we couldn't return to Honiara by ferry.

On our first day in Ringgi we had no luck searching for eagles but, on our second day, as we drove up the mountain, a large form flushed from the roadside and landed in a huge tree. It was a Solomon Sea Eagle that had been eating a dead possum on the road. Warily we got out of the truck to watch it and take photographs, the first, apparently, of the species. It flew up the hill into a clearing where we watched it for another two hours. Perched, and in flight, it looked very much like a White-bellied Sea Eagle only it was brown. White-bellied Sea Eagles occur in nearby Bismarck Archipelago but Solomon Sea Eagles take over from there, eastwards, and are the only eagles through the Solomons. Some ornithologists have suggested that the Solomon Sea Eagle is a subspecies of the White-bellied Sea Eagle and, though these taxonomic arguments between lumpers and splitters

generally don't matter much, this would mean we were looking at an endangered subspecies instead of an endangered
species.

The next day we travelled by canoe with Festus, a local forestry worker, to two islands in the area where he said there
had been eagles' nests. The first nest had been in a tall tree
in a mangrove swamp on Kohinggo Island, but it had fallen
down. There was no sign of recent use though we saw an
eagle soaring some three kilometres away towards the middle of this island. We were getting the impression that these
eagles were moving further and further from the coast to
escape persecution. Though Malaita has a substantial in-
land human population, the other major islands have their
human populations concentrated on the coast.

From there we travelled to Vonavona Island but the village
leader said the eagles that had nested above the village there
had been shot some time ago. He claimed that, in the past,
he watched eagles fly up and hold onto the trunk of a tree
outside a possum's hollow. The possum, thinking it was
night, came out and was caught by the eagle. Whether this
was a description of flushing behaviour we couldn't know.
Other raptors, like the Gymnogene, do fly up and hang onto
tree hollows but they use their double-jointed legs to reach
into hollows for prey. We had no way to verify this with
Solomon Sea Eagles. The man said that, in addition to pos-
sums and some fish, the eagles would chase the local dogs
and cats, which got the eagles into trouble. In many parts
of Australia an eagle that caught dogs and cats would be
praised.

The crossing back to Ringgi was stormy and, midway, the
motor pushing the dugout canoe died. Festus worked on it
for some time as we rocked in the open sea and, eventually,
got one of two pistons working. Limping on through the
storm, we reached Ringgi by nightfall.

We decided to return to Honiara and Guadalcanal by plane
the next day to explore some rivers there and see if we could

rent a helicopter to find an active nest, that is, one that contained eggs or young.

In Honiara we met Simon who knew of a nesting pair on Bonegi Creek just 10 kilometres west of Honiara. Simon led the way up Bonegi Creek for one and a half hours past villages, some gardens and through rich, green rainforest. One concern was the DDT used on Bonegi Creek. Malaria was a major problem on Guadalcanal, in fact it was said that they had the highest incidence in the world. As we watched, they sprayed huts, then rinsed, in Bonegi Creek, the metal canisters used to carry the chemicals. DDT would enter the waterways and we saw young boys hunting Black Ducks or fishing in the creek. This food went to their families.

As a further reminder of the DDT problem, but a very exciting one, I was amazed, as we came through a narrow gorge, to see a Peregrine flying over the tree canopy and down the hill. Peregrines weren't known to nest on Guadalcanal, though Mike McCoy, the local naturalist and photographer, said he had seen one in his garden, and the first breeding record could be an only record if DDT use continued. Simon said locals called the Peregrine 'Roja Bora' (Black Hawk) and that it dived swiftly on other birds and these birds greatly feared it.

Simon continued to lead us up Bonegi Creek to the point where the eagles had nested. But there was only a remnant bundle of sticks in the fork of a tree where the nest had been. We were disappointed to see a new village built directly across the creek from the nest. There had been a savage hurricane on the south-east side of Guadalcanal and some villagers had resettled from that ravaged landscape to Bonegi Creek. Further questioning revealed that the eagles may have been shot.

The following day we hired a helicopter to fly up the Lungga River and look for nests. The pilot, Dick Grouse, said he'd flown over one nest on Guadalcanal and this was a giant structure in the top of a giant rainforest tree over the mountains on the south side of the island. Dick was a former Viet Nam war pilot, familiar with exactly what could and couldn't be done with a helicopter and said that, if necessary, we could abseil into such a nest from his helicopter. The flight, with the doors off the helicopter, took us low over the rain-forest canopy. But we saw no eagles or nests.

The next day we flew out of Henderson field for Australia.

10 Canberra Falcons and Eagles

Canberra, the capital of Australia, is an exceptional city. The planners left forests and bushlands in and near the city and raptors breed there. Even eagles nest near suburbs and government buildings, and Peregrines nest in gorges and disused quarries.

The four of us reached the cliff after walking for an hour through brown-green forest and lichen-covered rock. Stephen Turner, my student at the University of Canberra, was finishing the third year of his science degree specialising in raptors. He is tall, strong and an excellent biologist. Alan Davies and Aidan Flannagan managed parts of the *Australian Capital Territory Forests* and had commissioned us to help them with a pair of Peregrines in one of their forests. This pair of falcons regularly failed and *A.C.T. Forests* wanted to know if they failed because of the walking trail that passed near the site carrying increased traffic each year. Five years of monitoring showed that the nest seldom fledged young. But factors other than human disturbance could cause failure, for example, the nest site could be accessible to foxes, or let in rain and storms. This nest, unfortunately, fit all three problem categories - it was close to a trail, humans and foxes could climb into it fairly easily, and, it was not protected from above or the sides by rock so rain storms could soak the nest and eggs or young.

105

We decided to check locations along the cliff where we could build, for these Peregrines, a new nest. The plan was to take a site they already roosted in, but couldn't nest in because it had sharp rocks or a slanting floor, level the floor and fill it with sand to provide a place for their eggs. It seemed that rain could pour into the first site we looked at, and soak any future young, so we decided to check a spot 30 feet further along the cliff. Because there was no tree directly above this next spot, we dragged the rope along the top, parallel to the cliff, looped it around a rock sticking out of the ground, and dangled the rope down over the spot. This was a serious mistake. I asked Stephen to hold the rope so it wouldn't slip off the rock but somehow there was miscommunication and I started down the cliff before Stephen was ready. The rope flipped off the rock and, with 30 feet of slack, I fell.

Hitting the end of the rope with a crunching jolt, I gripped hard to stop my dive to the bottom of the cliff. Suddenly my back crashed into a rock wall, then I was dreaming, pleasant dreams about walking and Peregrines and felt good.

Slowly waking, and they told me later I hadn't been out long, I looked around and had no idea why I lay on a rock ledge with a drop below me and I started to panic. Alan and Stephen yelled at me to tie myself to the rope so I wouldn't roll off the ledge into the gorge. It didn't register; I was too groggy, too disoriented. Finally, realising what they meant, I slowly and painfully tied myself to the rope to stop from rolling off the ledge. My co-ordination was hampered by the fracture in my back and a lacerated hand.

Stephen came down the rope to get me. After reaching the bottom of the cliff, with Stephen supporting me, we slowly climbed around to the top of the cliff and walked out of the gorge. Stephen, always conscientious, debated with me as we walked that it was his fault for not holding the rope; I said it was my fault for going too early.

We reached the cars and Stephen, Alan and Aiden drove me to the hospital where the real adventure started. A well-meaning nurse laid me on a clean white bed. It always feels uncomfortable to be so dirty in such a clean place. She started to remove the dirt from the lacerations on my right hand, the hand that stopped me from falling to the end of the rope. She scrubbed at my hand with a nail brush. The pain was too much and I told her to stop. She went looking for a doctor who could deaden the hand so she could clean out the debris driven in by the rope.

In came a pleasant, elderly man in a white coat, with a hypodermic in his right hand and a vial in his left. What happened next you may find a bit unbelievable. The doctor, swaying and shaking, brought the full hypodermic close to my hand, miscalculated, pricked himself through the rubber glove on his left hand, then continued with the momentum of his right hand into my laceration. He stuck himself, and, in the same movement, stuck me as if he couldn't stop the action once it started. To make things worse, he apologised and said it was the third time in as many months he'd done this so now we both needed to have AIDS and hepatitis tests. After climbing hundreds of trees, descending hundreds of cliffs for twenty-five years and trying to avoid attacking goshawks and falcons, it would be fitting to be killed by a hospital.

Peregrine Research

But it wasn't the end just yet and we returned to the Peregrine site some months later. Stephen crafted a nest from rock in the Peregrine roost I had fallen past but never reached. The pair had begun to scrape a depression for their eggs in the old, accessible and wet nest. But they preferred Stephen's ledge, protected from rain, foxes and most humans and moved straight in after we left, laid eggs in the following week and raised young for the first time in years.

Our decisions about these Peregrines that failed to raise young year after year, were based on field research. Solid research should, but often doesn't, underpin decisions about conserving and rehabilitating raptors. For example, many ornithologists believe that birds, including Peregrines, breed when prey is most abundant to feed their nestlings. So you would expect Galahs, European Starlings, rosellas and other birds that are the main prey of Peregrines near Canberra to peak in abundance and availability while Peregrines have nestlings in October and November. However, when we looked at the times when these prey birds fledged their own young and were most abundant for Peregrines to catch, we found this wasn't the case. Instead, these prey species were more available during January, February and March after young Peregrines fledge (Table 1).

Table 1
Fledging of Peregrines and Prey Species in Canberra 1984

	Aug	Sept	Oct	Nov	Dec	Jan	Feb	Mar
Starling			I————————I					
Galah				I————————I				
Crimson Rosella					I————————I			
Eastern Rosella					I————I			
Peregrine	I————I		I————I					
	hatch		fledge					

This makes sense when you watch young Peregrines learning to hunt. They try, but can't catch experienced adult prey. Young rosellas and other prey fledge about the same time or after young Peregrines fledge so young Peregrines learn to hunt this inexperienced prey. The lesson, then, was that young Peregrines that we hacked or fostered (see Appendix 1) would have the best chance of survival if we released them when they had abundant prey to learn to hunt. Also, if we had an injured raptor over the winter it may have trouble finding food in spring when prey numbers are lowest. It is more likely to survive in summer when prey numbers peak and there is inexperienced juvenile prey to hunt.

We also knew that Peregrines near Port Augusta and around Canberra fledged more young from nest sites that were protected from bad weather by overhanging rock, or were on cliffs that faced away from prevailing westerly storms. The size and success of a population of raptors is determined largely by two limited resources -food and nest sites. We knew the Canberra area had plenty of food in the form of parrots, starlings and other birds but there was a shortage of nest sites. Some Peregrines around Canberra nested on substandard cliffs. Those territories that had a quality nest site in a pothole, instead of on an unprotected ledge, fledged more young during rainy years (Table 2).

Table 2
Average Young Fledged per Territory From Nests in Potholes Compared to Nests on Ledges

Nest Type	Rainy Year	Dry Year
Ledge	0.91 young	1.43 young
Pothole	1.59 young	1.42 young

Those territories that had more than one suitable ledge to choose from, about a third of the Peregrine territories around Canberra, also fledged more young during rainy years than territories with only one available nest ledge (Table 3).

The poorer nest sites did better during drought years than during rainy years because they were less likely to be flooded. One year, after the young were gone, I poured a litre of water into each of these Canberra sites to see if drain-

109

age mattered. That is, would nests that drained well fledge more young in rainy years, but not during dry years, than nests that drained poorly? They did. Sites that drained better, fledged more young (Table 4).

Table 3

Average Young Fledged per Territory for Territories With More Than One Useable Nest Site Compared to Those With Only One Useable Nest Site

	One Useable Nest Site		More Than One Useable Nest Site	
	Rainy Year	Dry Year	Dry Year	Rainy Year
Yng per territ.	0.66	1.25	1.68	1.45
% terr. succes.	35%	61%	75%	75%

We knew what sort of Peregrine nest site would benefit the failing pair in the forest and we chose and modified the site to achieve better breeding results. We also knew that, on average, about 57% of Peregrine sites around Canberra fledge young in a year, about 43% fail or don't try, and that the average brood size was about 2.1 young each year. So we had a baseline; we knew how many young per year, on average, each pair should produce. We could look at Peregrine nests near walking trails and in nature parks and tell managers whether human disturbance was likely to be harming the breeding Peregrines.

It follows that orphaned and captive-bred young should be fostered into these good nests. That is, if we had young Peregrines brought to us, and they could be placed in a nest for wild parents to raise, we should choose nests that were inaccessible to humans and predators, 'weather-proof' and had a good record for fledging young. Then the extra young placed in the wild parents' care, and the original young that share the nest, had good chances of survival.

Table 4
Average Young Fledged per Territory From Nest Sites That Do Drain Compared to Nest Sites That Don't Drain

Average Young Fledged per Territory

Nest Ledge	Rainy Year	Dry Year
Drains	1.04 young	1.39 young
Doesn't Drain	0.72 young	1.43 young

Besides a good nest site, there is another important factor when fostering young raptors - ample food. Many ornithologists would argue, because of the work of David Lack and others, that wild raptors already have as many young as they can feed. That is, if they have a clutch size of three eggs, as do Peregrines in Australia, they have evolved to raise three young but not four or five young. A pair of Peregrines that laid only two eggs that year may only have the resources to raise two young. This means that if we put an extra young in their nest, and artificially increase their brood size to three, some young may go hungry. But we thought there was a 'buffer' of extra food that raptors didn't use. We thought they had extra food in their territory or home range to raise at least one extra young.

Fostering Wedge-tailed Eagles

With this argument in mind, David Mallinson, an ornithologist-botanist from the National Botanic Gardens, Sue Trost, a college teacher who helps with our field work, and I fostered some captive-bred Wedge-tailed Eagle chicks into wild nests and carefully monitored their progress. These chicks were bred at Taronga Park Zoo in Sydney and were older than any wild chicks we could find around Canberra. Sydney is coastal, lower in elevation, and warmer than Canberra so chicks in the zoo hatched earlier.

After surveying a number of nests near Canberra, David and I decided on two nests just over the border in New South Wales. The zoo chicks were still about two weeks older than the chicks already in these nests but we decided to try anyway. Captive-bred raptors that aren't fostered will sometimes languish in captivity or be traded to other zoos. Compared to flying the eagle and teaching it to hunt, fostering could be a superior type of release. Training the young eagle was time-consuming and could tame it to the point where it didn't fear humans, and was shot or sometimes attacked humans as conspecifics. A Wedge-tailed Eagle chick raised by wild eagles was more likely to socialise to other eagles than one trained by humans. Taronga Park Zoo is progressive and wanted their captive-bred eagles fostered into the wild.

Wedge-tailed Eagles have one, or sometimes, two chicks. A problem we faced, or more of a worry really, was that one of the nests we wanted to use already had two young. Would they be stretched for food if they had an unnatural brood size of three chicks in their nest?

David, Sue and I approached the bottom of the giant Casuarina on the banks of the Murrumbidgee River and tried again and again to get a rope 15 metres up over the first limb. We failed again and again until, finally, David tied one of our carabineers to a string and tossed it over the limb. We then tied the rope to the end of the string, pulled it over and tied the rope around David's waist and pulled him, half shinnying, up to the first limb. There he untied himself and would free-climb the next 20 metres to the nest. He tied some string to himself that followed him up the tree, snaking between the limbs. Sue and I then tied our end of this string to an empty feed sack and placed the young Wedge-tailed Eagle inside. David hauled it up, slowly and carefully so the bag, and the eagle it contained, wouldn't bang against the branches.

When the bag reached David at the nest, he carefully took the three-kilogram nestling out and placed it in the nest with its two, much smaller, foster-siblings. Taronga Park Zoo also gave us six large frozen rabbits, the natural food of Wedge-tailed Eagles. David placed them on the giant nest with the three eaglets. There was plenty of room for everybody.

David climbed down the tree and, because this nest was below an escarpment, we stood on top and looked in at the nestlings. The two downy residents sat still and eyed the newcomer but the zoo-bred eagle flapped its wings in the wind, held tightly to the nest with its talons, and generally gave the impression she felt good. She'd never been out of her cage at the zoo and had never been more than ten feet off the ground. She reacted quite naturally to the 50 metre high platform as if she had known those heights all her life.

That night there was a violent wind storm and I had nightmares. This eagle had no experience with high winds and, surely, she would blow out of the nest into the swift river and float away. That morning, with bags under my eyes, I went to check her from the escarpment above the nest. I needed to monitor three things - Did she blow away in the night? Was she bullying her younger and smaller foster-siblings? Was there extra food left in the nest, that is, were the adults able to feed three nestlings? She was there, not bullying her siblings, and they had extra food on the nest. We checked the nest every day for two weeks until the zoo-bred eagle fledged. Always there was extra food on the nest and never did we see evidence of fighting. All three nestlings grew accustomed to each other and fledged normally.

We suspected that one reason these eagles had abundant food was their proximity to houses and humans. Graziers shot and poisoned Wedge-tailed Eagles in the thousands for many years. However, education and legislation reduced this killing during the 1980's. Most eagles remained wary of humans, stayed out of rifle range and nested far from houses. But that started to change in the late 1980's and David Mallinson found a territory reoccupied by Wedge-tailed Eagles near Canberra suburbs after a 10 year absence. They usurped the resident Little Eagles and there were so few pairs of eagles close by that they probably had all the rabbits to themselves. In the future, we may not be able to increase broods of Wedge-tailed Eagles from two to three if they start to recolonise their former territories and their food supply becomes more of a limiting resource.

Fostering Peregrines

We had placed nestling captive-bred Peregrines into nests of wild Peregrines several times and these chicks, and their nest-mates, always fledged successfully. We even had one return to Canberra a year later and strike a wire. We released him after he recovered, 48 hours later. Stephen, Sue and I decided to look more carefully at the question of artificially increasing broods of Peregrines, by adding extra young, and monitoring how adults cope with these extra young. We removed two female 21-day-old nestlings from a nest where, in previous years, young had been killed by storms, and placed each female in a different new nest that already had three young. This left the first nest with one young, the second nest with four young (the original three plus an introduced extra) and the third nest with four young (the original three plus an introduced extra). At 35 days old we returned the females to their original nests and continued to monitor all the nests. We also monitored two other nests - one that had three young and one that had two. When I say 'monitor' these five nests, what we actually did was measure and weigh the young at each nest twice a week and collect prey remains for analysis. Therefore, we could see if the young in the increased broods of four started to lose weight when we placed extra young there at 21 days old or if they started to gain weight after we put them back. By monitoring prey remains we could determine if prey brought to the nest increased before, during, or after we fostered young. That is, we could tell, when we added an extra chick, whether parents increased the amount of food brought to the nest so all chicks received ample food.

In short, we found, firstly, that none of the five broods had different growth rates, except, for some odd reason, the broods we increased to four grew faster than the broods we didn't increase. It seemed that the parents started to bring in extra food to compensate for the extra young we put in their nests and went a bit overboard. We also found that the parents of these larger broods didn't actually bring more of the same prey type, they caught larger prey species after we placed the extra young with them. So the parents caught birds like European Starlings and rosellas that weigh about 100 grams each before we increased their broods from three to four. After we increased their broods to four, the parents caught larger birds that weighed about 300 grams each, like Galahs, Silver Gulls and other larger birds.

Raptors like Peregrines, with females larger than males, tend to have the female stay with the chicks and guard them while the male hunts. We thought that, when the extra chicks were introduced to their nests, the females must have started to hunt these larger prey species in a 'prey refuge' near the nest so they could still guard the young.

So it seems that some raptors can compensate for extra young placed in their nests by catching larger prey species. However this may be at some cost to the adults, especially females, because they have more risk of accident while hunting and they use more energy. This is yet to be studied.

Switching Mother Peregrines

Conventional thinking about Peregrines is that males are the hunters and females are the care-givers in the raptor pair. But, as we thought happened with the broods increased to four, the hunting prowess of females could be important for the survival of nestlings in most nests. Further clues came from our observations at another Peregrine site. Libby Stevenson, a student from the University of Canberra, watched a Peregrine pair during courtship through incubation and the nestling phase, until the young fledged. Libby was an excellent and meticulous field researcher who, though she is slight, carried a giant pack full of equipment down the hill twice a week, to watch the Peregrine pair, and carried it back up the hill afterwards.

Everything went according to expectations with Libby's data collection until close to hatching time. This female Peregrine had been screaming for food most days; she obviously was hungry and the male wasn't feeding her enough. Sometimes she went off hunting on her own and left the male on the eggs. Around hatching time, she disappeared (she was banded), and was replaced by a new (larger, unbanded) female. We didn't know whether the original female left, hurt herself while hunting, or met some other fate. This new female hatched the eggs and began to brood and raise the young. She became a foster mother and raised a brood of three chicks that weren't hers.

But the new female also screamed for food and the male didn't seem to feed her any better than his first mate. Stephen or I roped down to the ledge every three days to measure the young and collect prey remains and, when the young were about 22 days old, I grew concerned about their welfare. The male continued to bring in small prey, like Starlings, but not enough of them. It seemed as though the chicks could starve.

As we had to make a decision, I met with Libby and Stephen. The chicks' growth rate continued to fall so they soon would be in danger. Should we feed them or let nature take its course and, perhaps, let them die? This may seem like a straightforward problem for anyone involved in raptor rehabilitation - Peregrines have enough trouble as it is, we should help them out. But we decided not to feed them. We needed to learn more about how males and females interact to raise their young and divide duties. What Libby was recording was, we thought, quite natural, so we wouldn't help the young until things were critical.

The male continued to bring starlings and rosellas, but not enough to keep his family going and, one day, the female started to hunt and bring larger prey to the nest like Magpies, Galahs, and Spur-winged Plovers. The nestling weights rose up into the normal range and they fledged normally. The female's hunting competence, and her ability to bring in larger prey, seemed to have saved the male's family for him, and for us. Males may compete for the limited resource of a competent female that can hunt in a 'prey refuge' near the nest and, also, care for the young.

We have much to learn about fostering, rehabilitation and the conservation of raptors. To conserve a raptor we need to study its basic ecology. The new generation of ecologists, like Libby Stevenson and Stephen Turner, know a good place to start - sitting near a raptor nest watching dramas unfold through a telescope.

11 Back in the U.S.A.

April 1993 and, after 21 years, it was good to sit in Les Boyd's living room again. He was the same - charitable with falcons and people. Alan Gardner comes to visit and we laugh about trapping falcons and backing into police cars and the expensive obsession we had more than 20 years ago. So, how much has changed? We all have some grey hair but all three of us still live with falcons. Professionally we've gone different directions. Alan works as an engineer repairing water tanks and the like. Les has quit his job at Washington State University and set up a business, with his son Chris, breeding Peregrines for falconers and for release into the wild where Peregrines are extinct. They also breed and sell Coturnix Quail to feed these falcons.

Like he did 21 years ago, Les offers me a room for three months while I'm on sabbatical at Washington State University. We plan road trips for the weekends through spring and summer to see Washington, Idaho and Montana, the land, raptors and some people. As if there was no twenty-one years since our last trips, the passion for raptors and their country, the restless urge to search, is still there.

In the morning Les shows me his raptor and quail breeding project. It's housed in a cluster of huge barns where falcons have enough room to fly back and forth and feel free. This, according to Les, helps the male to do his part.

Opinions differ in America about whether falcons should be sold or not. Australians are very much against selling any wildlife. American culture, with its anti-socialist foundations and its belief in the individual, differs from Australia. Kerouac and Hemingway taught us about the individual, the good things about self-reliance, and they reflected American values. For example, when inflation caused 1 cent coins to be almost valueless in Australia, the government spent massive public funds taking them out of circulation and replacing them with other coinage. In America, businesses like grocery stores, instead, put small trays at counters where you could put any 1 cent coins you have. The next person to come along could take 1 cent pieces for small change to make up his or her purchase. Individuals, not big government, solved the problem. It is said that the Civil War shaped the psyche of the American people but the American Revolution really shaped it. They threw off the bonds of large, oppressive government that taxed them without representation, a government that interfered too much in their commerce and daily lives.

So, many Americans had trouble understanding Australia. Some expressed anger that the Australian government was so restrictive about selling common parrots like Galahs and Sulphur-crested Cockatoos. Why couldn't they sell them to Americans who wanted them instead of allowing farmers in Australia to shoot them? I couldn't answer that easily but could see how the two cultures, and I include New Zealand with Australia, wouldn't understand each other on some wildlife issues. New Zealand Falcons, for example, came out of New Zealand on the understanding that they would be used for research and become part of an off-shore, captive-bred gene pool. But, soon after, North American and British falconers could buy the captive-bred progeny of these original pairs and use them to hunt British and American quarry. American falconers were completely bewildered as to why this annoyed some New Zealanders. Some Australian Peregrines are also available in the United States as falconry birds.

Pheasants, Hungarian Partridges and other introduced game birds were managed and protected in the United States. Introduced species, 'feral animals' if you like, were protected from native species like Coyotes which could be shot if accused of killing these introduced game birds. The hunting culture controls much in the United States and drives the powerful gun lobby that we, in Australia, hear so much about. Hunters and governments see these introduced game animals as having more rights than some native animals because the game species have value to hunters and economic value to arms and ammunition manufacturers. At a conservation meeting at the University of Idaho I annoyed some wildlife experts by questioning why they placed Pheasants in a conservation brochure and why these 'feral' animals were protected at all. Pheasants, Turkeys and California Quail occur in Australia and are unprotected feral animals there. The response was that introduced game birds had been in America for so long that, now, they were considered part of the ecology. These biologists were very protective of these 'feral' species, as some members of the Australian public are protective about feral horses or deer.

In this hunting culture Les set up his business. He had 12 pairs of Peregrines, mostly Barbary Falcons, a distinct subspecies from North Africa. All twelve pairs produced young while I was there because Les could coax each individual pair to breed by nurturing, careful feeding and monitoring. He hatched most of the eggs in incubators set up near his kitchen and, when each egg pipped and chicks would emerge within 48 hours, he held the eggs up to listen for the nestling's cheep then he cheeped back to them so they'd know his voice. When he fed them tiny bits of meat in their first days after hatching, he could get each chick to open its mouth and beg by giving his 'cheep' call. He was very gentle and maternal with each chick and raised it with care so it felt secure. This, Les said, would stop it from screaming for food as it grew into a juvenile. Screaming is a particularly annoying trait that falconers dislike.

Les also had some pairs of Peale's Falcons, the largest type of Peregrine, and these went out to hack sites, in places like

Missouri, to re-establish Peregrines where they were extinct. As you would expect, the politics around Peregrines and the release of Peregrines back into North America were volatile. Les had tried to release some onto the Grande Rond River near the Washington-Oregon border but was stopped, apparently by the Peregrine Fund, who were the main group releasing Peregrines in the United States. The reasons were about genetics, and this is where taxonomy becomes important. The Peregrine occurs world wide but isn't endangered world wide. Only some of the 17 or so subspecies are endangered and these are the subspecies that conservationists try to save. There is no need for such a programme in Australia because there was only localised eggshell thinning from DDT and some localised persecution, but the subspecies *Falco peregrinus macropus* was, as a whole, not endangered. The main Peregrine subspecies in the United States outside of Alaska is *Falco peregrinus anatum* and it was endangered. In fact, it disappeared altogether east of the Mississippi River and that was the problem. *Falco pereginus anatum* occurred sparingly west of the Mississippi but not east of the Mississippi. It was extinct there. So the Peregrine Fund got other Peregrine subspecies, like *F.p. brookei,* that was still common in Spain, and *F.p. pealei*, the Peale's Falcon from the west coast of Canada and southern Alaska, bred these in captivity with some *F.p. anatum* and other subspecies, then released the young into the eastern United States where Peregrines were extinct. This drew howls from some purists who argued that *F.p. anatum*, and not foreign subspecies, should be released there. Nobody, it was decided, could release Peregrines other than *F.p. anatum* west of the Mississippi where a few still bred.

So Les readied some of his Peregrine chicks for release in Missouri where non-*anatum* subspecies, and mixtures of subspecies, could be released. We took a downy nestling female in to Washington State University where Eric Stauber, an old friend who taught in the veterinary school there, could examine the chick and organise health certificates for her to travel interstate for release. Eric runs a highly successful raptor rehabilitation program at the University and gives excellent talks to high school students using unreleasable hawks, owls and falcons. He, and the hawks and owls held on his gloved fist, kept the students' attention for hours. Eric passed the Peregrine chick on its health exam so we could transport it to Spokane Airport and place it on the next flight to Missouri. There she'd be placed in a hack box with other nestling Peregrines (see Appendix 1) and they would learn to hunt together. Les was always careful that these Peregrines sent out for release had been raised by their parents, not by humans, so they were socialised to other Peregrines and would eventually breed in the wild.

In the following week, another nestling, a male, went through the same process - taken from its parents in Les's loft, passed through Eric Stauber's clinic at W.S.U. for a health certificate, then sent by air to Missouri where it was placed under a pair of Peregrines on a building that had laid infertile eggs. The pair accepted and raised Les's captive-bred nestling and it fledged successfully to face the stern hardships of nature. If the Peregrine survived for three or four years, and most don't because accidents, starvation, humans or other predators kill them, then he could return to the place where he was released, or a place like it, attract a mate, and breed.

One of our first road trips that spring was to Boise, Idaho, some eight hours away, and the Mecca of falcon authorities. We had three friends there - Tom Cade and Bill Burnam at the Peregine Fund and World Center for Birds of Prey, and Bruce Haak, a biologist and falconer with Idaho Fish and Game. The trip down through the Nez Pierce Indian Reservation, Riggins and the Salmon River Gorge took us into abundant wild country and reminded us how natural and empty Idaho was. There were few roads through much of its mountainous centre.

Boise is in a dry, wide valley skirted by sagebrush and rolling hills. Nearby is the Snake River Birds of Prey Area that hosts more breeding raptors, mainly Prairie Falcons, Red-tailed Hawks, Golden Eagles, Ferruginous Hawks and Turkey Vultures, than any place on earth. Morlan Nelson, a falconer and conservationist who helped with a number of early Walt Disney wildlife films, worked hard to protect the area as a reserve. It now boasts more raptor research than anywhere in the world. Les and I visited the reserve with Mike Kochert, who co-ordinates research in the area for the U.S. Bureau of Land Management. The day was uncharacteristically rainy as we travelled through sagebrush to the lip of the giant canyon. The main prey base for raptors there is the Townsend's Ground Squirrel which lives in prodigious numbers on the flats above the canyon. We travelled down a winding, dirt road cut into the side of the canyon to its floor. From the bottom of the canyon we saw, and heard, dozens of Prairie Falcons flying back and forth from their nests, up over the 300 metre canyon wall to the sagebrush flats above and returning to their nests with prey for their begging young.

We visited a Prairie Falcon eyrie then a Golden Eagle nest where we found the young had jumped out and were crouched beside rocks below. Mike explained that nestling raptors, especially Prairie Falcons in the canyon, were harassed by a blood-sucking ectoparasite, rather like a bedbug, that irritated them and, because of this, some nestlings leave the nest prematurely. Those Prairie Falcons that use a bare dirt ledge, for no falcons build there own nest, had less infestation than those using the stick nest of a raven, eagle or hawk. Stick nests, he explained, may harbour more of the parasites than bare earth. We chased one young eagle across the sagebrush-covered hill to catch him and place him in a safer spot. As we cornered him against a rock wall, he bolted past us down the hill, for nestling eagles can run surprisingly fast, and tumbled in the rock scree below. We caught and photographed him, then placed him further up the hill. The adult eagles would find him there and feed him and he'd be safer from coyotes and dogs. They were very much like nestlings of Australian Wedge-tailed Eagles.

We travelled back up and out of the canyon onto the sagebrush plains to watch some Prairie Falcons hunt, then drove to a Ferruginous Hawk nest on a power pylon. The power authority had built metal shelves into some of these poles on the treeless plain and Ferruginous Hawks, which normally nest on the ground there, moved in to build nests. In parts of Australia, raptors are given no such help as workers see their nests as a nuisance, and, in some regions, nests with young are thrown from the power pylons.

These hawks flew over us with strong wingbeats and soared and called, bright white in the Idaho sun. They were similar to Australian Little Eagles but larger, with more falcon-like flight and more pointed wings. Ferruginous hawks are mammal specialists and, with Golden Eagles, are the only raptor strong enough to catch the local White-tailed Jack Rabbits which, really, are big hares. Mike had kindly set out to show us a good day and succeeded admirably.

The next day we visited the Peregrine Fund and World Center for Birds of Prey, and its director Bill Burnam the President and Director. Tom Cade, the Founding Chairman and Director of the Center had left for Alaska, so Bill kindly showed us his massive organisation. The Peregrine Fund and World Center for Birds of Prey are a rambling set of structures built in sagebrush on a hill above Boise and are one of the great success stories in the raptor world. They have released some four and a half thousand Peregrines into the wild and drawn some $2,000,000 from gifts, interest, grants and sales in 1992.

Not only did Bill and Tom help save the Peregrine in North America but they developed a particular brand of entrepreneurship that generated millions of dollars to help birds of prey. Notables like Roy Disney had been on their executive board and, in addition, Bill and Tom used the selling power of the Peregrine. They attracted millions of dollars and ran their organisation without public funding. Expert advisers, like Les, had helped improve their captive breeding techniques and helped with publicity.

Bill showed us their new education centre where films would show and speakers come in, sometimes with a Peregrine on their gloved fist, to teach the public about raptors, ecology and the work of the Center. Through reflective glass we could see the giant breeding aviaries of Harpy Eagles. These massive birds live in endangered South American rainforest. Bill proudly showed us a number of electronic educational tools like a giant fibre-optic map where you pressed a button over the species that interested you and could see its migration light up in waves of light on the map.

The World Center's success with captive breeding had been such that they'd been asked to help with the endangered Hawaiian Crow, a handful of which live on a single ranch in Hawaii. They agreed to help and, Bill said, they had since been asked to help with smaller endangered passerines. This, he said, was a dilemma. They had to decide how far away from raptors their work could develop. Traditionally, all involved with the Center were raptor specialists, especially falconers.

While in Boise, we also visited John Marzluff, the Director of Greenfalk, a research organisation specialising in Prairie Falcons in the Snake River Birds of Prey Area. He explained the scope and breadth of their field research and showed us their captive crow colony. They would study ways to release young Common Crows into the wild before trying, with Bill Burnam's team, to breed, and release back into the wild, the endangered Hawaiian Crow.

In Boise Bruce Haak, with his wife Evelyn's editing expertise, recently published *The Hunting Falcon* and soon would publish *Prairie Falcon: Pirate of the Plains*. Bruce worked for Idaho Fish and Game and showed us, one rainy afternoon, the Morrison Knudson Nature Center that his service was building in central Boise. They took a block of disused ground, fashioned a creek running through it, a pond, trees, local plants and showed people how they could change parts of their farm, or even their yard, to better see and protect wildlife. The stream cut a cross-section through parts of the interpretation centre so visitors could see into the running stream from the side and view the breeding cycle of several species of fish. The mini-environment was an excellent example of reclaiming degraded city land so it became valuable wildlife habitat.

Inside the interpretation centre one wall had some thirty porcelain tiles, each painted with an animal, like White-tailed Deer, Black Bear or Peregrine Falcon, on them. Each tile also had the name of a company or a person who had contributed money to the Center. These people, therefore, were given identity and a sense of ownership for their part in building the Center. The Americans, not surprisingly, know how to sell and how to generate funds to the point where institutions like the World Center for Birds of Prey and the Morrison-Knudson Nature Center can be built and run mainly from private funds. We, from countries that expect governments to develop such programs for us, could learn, from the Americans, how to build programs from private funds.

On our next trip we visited Coeur d'Alene Lake to meet with Don Johnson, a raptor ecologist with the University of Idaho. He studied Ospreys on the giant lake and invited us to band adults with him. Don is a big, grey-haired man still active in the field at 62, and he did the sort of field work we enjoyed. We boated out onto the lake towards a number of pilings left from old bridges. It was astounding. During my boyhood the Ospreys were reduced on this lake, some 20 miles from my home, to a few dozen. But they had exploded in recent years to hundreds of pairs. They nested on the old pilings and even some distance away from the lake on telephone poles.

Why had a raptor considered endangered in parts of the U.S. experienced such an explosion in numbers here? Don saw the change in terms of education and legislation. DDT had thinned their eggs, stopping many from breeding, and people had shot them indiscriminately, not only because they were 'hawks' but also because fishermen believed they took fish that anglers wanted. The government legislated against DDT and shooting Ospreys and taught the public to value and conserve these fine hunters. People were lucky to have Ospreys to watch. It worked. Shooting was greatly reduced, and Ospreys came back in huge numbers.

Don boated up to each piling containing a nest and flushed the incubating bird, usually the female, from its eggs. Then we braced a ladder in the boat and leaned it against the piling. Les or I climbed up the ladder and placed a wire-mesh cone covered with monofilament nooses, like on a bal-cha-tri, over the eggs. This was tied, with twine, underneath the nest like a bonnet. We climbed down the ladder and boated off some 100 metres to watch with binoculars. Some-times the Osprey stayed away from its eggs for ten or fif-teen minutes but, then, either the male or female came and tried to sit on the eggs. They walked around on the cone trying to get to their eggs until, finally, they entangled their feet in the nooses. We watched and, when the Osprey tried to fly up but pulled the trap up with it, we knew they were caught. Then we started the motor and moved quickly to the nest and set the ladder. One of us climbed up, retrieved the Osprey, untangled its feet and brought it down to the boat to be banded and released. Sometimes, while we had the female, the male would go over to incubate the eggs and we caught him.

The trap was old with nooses weakened by use. A number of females we caught that day struggled, broke the nooses and escaped. This was a problem because it left them shy of the trap and difficult to retrap. Some nests were only 200 metres apart so we simply travelled from one to the other. It was very easy work compared to the long walks, climbs and distances that raptor biologists face in Australia. We were grateful to Don for sharing his work with us and heart-ened by the success story of Lake Coeur d'Alene's Ospreys.

Les and I next travelled up through Lolo Pass, the pass where Chief Joseph of the Nez Pierces, with his people, led a brilliant tactical retreat and did it with such speed and skill that the U.S. Army failed to keep up. The forest and mountains along the Loohsa River leading into the pass are wild and rich. We dropped down into Lolo and Missoula, the towns Norman Maclean wrote so elegantly about in *A River Runs Through It*. After a night in Soho, we travelled north to meet Dale Becker, the biologist for the Confeder-ated Salish and Kootenai Tribes of the Flathead Nation.

Dale showed us a number of raptors on the Flathead Indian Reservation. They were particularly pleased that Bald Eagles had returned to breed in numbers, and they were re-establishing Peregrines supplied by the World Center for Birds of Prey. There were many sites of Prairie Falcons, Golden Eagles and other raptors.

Les and I were particularly impressed with the conservation skills of Indian tribes in the northwest, including those from the Flathead Nation and the Quinalts in Washington. While Steelhead and other fish stocks declined, the Quinalts, on Washington's Olympic Peninsula, managed theirs well so ample stocks remained for fishing. At Inchelium, on the Colville Indian Reservation in Washington, tribal members logged and had recreational businesses, like houseboats for hire on Lake Roosevelt, that generated income for all tribal members, including children. But the forests and lakes there were as beautiful and well managed in 1993 as they had been during the 1960's. Here on the Flathead Indian Reservation the Tribal Council had clear management guidelines based on conservation of the land, its forests and animals, including a buffalo herd. They saw the environment holistically and felt a sense of long-term ownership. This relationship to the land meant they managed it better than their white counterparts on privately owned land. We left the reservation wondering if white landowners would learn from their Indian neighbours.

One final trip. We reached the Prairie Falcon eyrie on Rock Lake, a beautiful desert lake that, historically, was much feared by the Palouse Indians who thought it was bottomless and contained dangerous creatures. The pristine, white, male falcon perched, like a perfect china figurine on a rock pinnacle above the nest. The female wasn't visible and there were no people. It was quiet except for swallows, swifts and some gulls and we could see Turkey Vultures and Red-tailed Hawks soaring silently above. We pulled the boat up to the shore and hiked up the hill to a level above the cliff, then left over to the top of the cliff. There were no trees in the sagebrush there so we did what we did 21 years ago. Les wrapped the rope around his waist and sat down in a small depression. He dug his feet into the ground between two sweet-smelling Sagebrush bushes and said, "O.K., go ahead, I'm set."

Standing on the edge of the cliff, I leaned back on the rope tied in with a carabineer and 8-ring to the sling, and abseiled down to the nest. I knew Les would hold me. At the nest I examined prey remains while the female, who suddenly returned, swooped in at me. She was perfect and sandy like the desert. The remains seemed to be mainly birds including Western Meadowlarks, Horned Larks and Chukar Partridges, quite a large bird for Prairie Falcons to catch and carry to the nest. Also I photographed the four downy white nestlings with their growing feathers and made comparisons with Peregrines back home. They were similar in size and their down was the same pure white, but the light sandy colour of their feathers and grey legs (nestling Peregrines in Australia have yellow legs and dark feathers) made them different. They were gentler and less vocal than our Peregrines which struggled and grabbed us. The nestlings flipped onto their backs and hissed like falcons everywhere. They were alluring and perfect. To visit them high in their eyrie was both new and nostalgic.

After roping to the bottom, I carried the equipment back up and around to the top of the cliff for Les. I dug myself into the same position between the two fragrant sagebrush plants and Les tied himself onto the rope. He leaned back at the top of the cliff and went down to view the nest.

To the Indians, Rock Lake was a sacred place and, sometimes, a place to fear. On the way home, Les said the visit to the eyrie on the quiet, sagebrush hill was close to a spiritual experience. I guess it was.

12 Refuge

An injured female Sparrowhawk sits at my feet. It looks like she may die. Lying in the bottom of a box unable to stand, unable to feed, her eyes closed, a lovely brown and sepia hawk with long skinny toes used to snatch birds out of mid-air. She smells sweet and clean, and a little of formic acid from ants she has crushed through her feathers. I told the man who brought her that she may not last the night. Her black pupils dilate and contract rapidly and wildly in her lemon-yellow eyes.

A quick examination; no broken bones, no blood or sign of disease anywhere. These Sparrowhawks fly in low and fast to dodge around bushes and fences and use this cover to ambush small birds. She might have some disease but, more likely, she hit a car or some object while hunting. The flesh on her sternum is round, she's not starving. But there seems to be some neurological damage. She can't stand and she acts totally confused and gazes around the room with her head on its side. She fears nothing.

Sparrowhawks die easily from stress. Too much handling, including this examination, could kill her. So I keep the examination brief and place her in a darkened box to sleep. No attempt to feed her now; she's not strong enough to be force-fed and she can't feed herself.

Day two
She's very sick and needs to be force-fed. Just lies in the bottom of the box with her eyes closed. By holding her in my left hand I can open her beak with my right hand and force an aspirin-sized piece of beef into the back of her mouth. She struggles and I hate using force, feel guilty and wonder if it's worth it. But pieces are repeatedly forced down her until their is a small bulge at her throat. Otherwise, she'll die within a few days. This is about an eighth of a crop and will do for now. If she gets more, she could become stressed or vomit up a fuller crop. She closes her yellow eyes soon after, gives up struggling and lies in the bottom of the box.

Day three
Her lemon-yellow eyes blink open but, then, she closes them again. Another series of force-feeds like yesterday with one late at night before I go to bed. I don't want to do this any more; it depresses me. The motivation is, in part, to help because she's our weakened brethren and her injuries most likely came from us. We owe her. But also the motivation is to avoid the hurt of loss, bereavement and failure if she dies. To avoid guilt.

Day four
She looks much the same and, when I feel her sternum, I'm alarmed at how thin she is. She's losing weight fast. My stomach starts to knot as I remember injured hawks we lost. They started down like this and no amount of work could save them. Sick with worry, and the prospect of failure, I take her to work. The staff and students at the university are always kind about these rehabilitation cases and want to help with her. She can be fed every three hours at work and get as much beef fat as she'll take. If she continues to weaken and lose condition, her normal parasite load could increase and drag her further down. She could reach a point where she can't come back up and she'll die.

Day five
She's stronger and sits on her knees in the corner of the cardboard box. Her vision is blurred and she pecks at things in mid-air, things that aren't there. She can, however, see

the small pieces of red meat held before her and she begins to take them from my fingers. She no longer needs to be force-fed, the stress is reduced for her and for me. Force-feeding, the stress of holding her and forcing food down her throat, would eventually have killed her and dispirited me.

Day six

I take her out of the box and stand her on a piece of news-print. Four feedings today on small pieces of beef that she takes from my fingers. She can stand now and her eyes are somewhat clearer but still she pecks at imaginary pieces in mid-air and still she wants to lie down and close her eyes after five or so minutes. I place a pile of small pieces of meat 10 centimetres away from her and she walks over and picks them up, slowly one by one. Another small triumph. Maybe she will live.

Day seven

My 15-year-old daughter, Anna, is with me and my friend Ian Warden visits with his 16-year-old son Zach. The Sparrowhawk has been in a box all night so I gently lift her out and put her on the newspaper. She can't co-ordinate her feet but we need to push her each day, get her to try some-thing new. I warn my guests that she's ill and can't do much. Perhaps a bit defensive, a bit protective towards her, like protecting one's children from harm and derision. Ian and Anna hold small pieces of meat to her beak which she eats. Zach declines and the teenagers glance awkwardly at each other. The Sparrowhawk takes pieces of raw steak gently from their fingers and continues to reach for imaginary pieces above her. She is gentle and endearing. Ian places a larger piece, too large to swallow, 10 centimetres away from her and she walks to it and lifts it up in her beak over and over but drops it every time. She can't seem to co-ordinate her feet to hook them into the meat. Raptors hook their talons into their prey and lean down and hook their beaks into the object, pulling upwards with their leg and back muscles. They tear off these small pieces and flick them back into their throat and swallow them. The Sparrowhawk tries this manoeuvre eight or ten times with my guests watching but she fails each time. But then, after this perseverance, she gets her talons hooked into the meat and pulls off a piece with her beak, then swallows it. Another triumph, and we all smile. Maybe she'll live and maybe she can go back to the wild. But she can suffer reversals and die or plateau and remain an invalid in captivity as others have. We anticipate tomorrow with clear goals and some optimism.

Day eight
Her eye is clear and yellow and bright and she stands comfortably on one leg. A good sign because raptors at ease usually rest on one, not two, legs. Most birds prefer to stand on one leg, a stance that most people attribute to herons and storks. My son Peter remarks on how tame she is, showing no fear of us at all. Is she partially blind or just trusting? To test her vision I take her in the bathroom to see her own reflection in the mirror. Nothing at first. But then she flares the hackles on her neck and spreads her wings in threat. Peter laughs. We're heartened that she's ready to fight the enemy in the mirror.

Day nine
She's the same. The dramatic change for the better over the past week has slowed or, perhaps, stopped. Her vision still seems blurred and sometimes she can't see the meat placed on her perch. Perhaps she's ignoring it. Time for another test. I push my hand behind her legs. She steps back and I lift her and take her to the mirror. At first she does nothing, she ignores her own reflection. Then as I move her closer to the mirror, she suddenly spreads her wings and fluffs out all her feathers in threat. She's so disturbed by her own image that she leaps off my hand and glides to the floor. She can't fly and one wing hangs when she spreads it. The Sparrowhawk waits for me to pick her up and return her to the perch on my living room floor.

Day ten
No change, though she eats well and roosts mainly on one leg. She's still very tired and sleeps most of the day while people rush around the house over and around her. For some reason she still has great difficulty hooking her talons into the food and reaching down to tear off pieces with her beak.

She may never again master flying because it takes far more co-ordination and synchronisation to fly than to pull off pieces of food and swallow them. But she may have been hit by a car and, like anyone hit by a car, she's stiff with her injuries. So I help her by tearing off small pieces of steak. We've learned to live together, but it's time for her to leave. She needs an outside flight pen so I phone Frank and Tanya, my friends on the river, to take her.

Day 11
They come late in the evening and I pick her up on my hand to show them how tame and trusting she is, how she'll eat meat from their fingers while perched there. They take her to their car in a cardboard box and Frank says he'll keep me posted on her progress. Some lament but mainly hope.

Day 15
Frank telephones, worried. The Sparrowhawk can eat and take food from his fingers but sometimes loses her balance and falls off her perch in the flight cage. He fears she has permanent brain damage. She'll never go and will always be caged.

Day 25
Frank telephones. She's made rapid progress in the last 10 days and can fly around the cage. He's excited and pleased with his work. We make plans to release her.

Day 50
With each report from Frank the Sparrowhawk is stronger, eating better, moulting (usually a sign of health) and closer to release. Because the prey species she pursues tend to peak in abundance during late summer, we decide to release her in March.

There's a small ceremony on top of Mount Ainslie where Bill Wood, the Minister for the Environment, holds the hawk before casting her skyward. The television news and *Canberra Times* watch and ask questions; the media has an enormous capacity for this stuff. Perhaps it matters little in the larger scheme of things, but it's a small triumph to accompany this delicate hawk from near death to release. We're quiet and gratified as we see her circle high and disappear.

Appendix 1
Handbook for Rehabilitating
Orphaned and Injured Raptors

Many people each year find injured raptors that fly into wires or cars, and orphaned nestlings that fall from nests or are taken by people as pets. Most of us would like these raptors returned to the wild but often they continue their run of bad luck and die or end up permanently captive because well-meaning people don't know how to adequately care for them.

By law, the appropriate wildlife authority* should be notified if you find or receive an injured or orphaned raptor. In Australia their officers will refer you to established wildlife parks, or to voluntary rehabilitation organisations, like W.I.R.E.S. in Sydney or the Wildlife Foundation in Canberra or to other licensed individuals competent and willing to care for raptors. Unfortunately, many wildlife parks are shutting down or, because of their special requirements, authorities won't allow them to keep raptors. At the time of writing, far more injured and orphaned raptors are found than there are willing and competent people to care for them. As a result, many raptors are euthanized or die in captivity, or they remain in captivity for too long or they are released without a proper assessment of their chances of survival. Stress, inadequate food, improper housing and premature release kill many of these raptors. They often aren't fed enough, or they are caged inadequately. When disturbed in this housing, they thrash in fear back and forth against the wire walls, break feathers and damage their beak and cere. You can imagine the terror that dogs, inquisitive children and looming faces strike in a recently injured or orphaned raptor.

Birds of prey will, of course, have a much better chance of survival if you have some knowledge of their proper care. Raptors are adapted to an environment where they have a balanced diet, a wide choice of perches, freedom from disturbance, and access to sun, water, wind, heat and cold. Three books - *Veterinary Aspects of Captive Birds of Prey* 1978 by John Cooper, *The Hawk Trust*, Newent, Glos. England, *Medical Management of Birds of Prey* 1993 by Patrick Redig, Raptor Center at the University of Minnesota, St Paul MN, and *Caring for Birds of Prey* 1990 by Jerry Olsen, Wild Ones, Springville California, and University of Canberra can help your rehabilitation effort. A brief summary of the essentials for successful rehabilitation follows:

GUIDELINES FOR CARERS

Picking Up Injured or Orphaned Raptors

Falcons, and most raptors, have very powerful feet and talons and only slightly less powerful beaks. When you hold them, they can struggle violently and break their feathers, hurt themselves or injure you. By following the steps listed below you can avoid these dangers:

1. Firstly throw a towel or jacket over the falcon. This should cover its head and engage, rather than entangle its claws, and

2. Place a hand in the middle of the raptor's back and press down so that its legs extend backwards out under its tail. Then encircle the body, including the wings and legs, by wrapping both hands around the raptor's lower back just above where the tail feathers emerge (Figure 1).

3.   Carefully disengage the raptor's claws from the towel or jacket and place the bird in a darkened cardboard box. Keep the bird cool.

Caring for Young Raptors

Try to avoid hand-raising a raptor. If no wild or captive adults are available for fostering, then hand raising may be necessary. But special care is necessary for the chick to be suitable for release.

Avoiding Imprinting

It is crucial to avoid taming raptors or imprinting them to humans. Nestlings between about two weeks and four weeks old can imprint to humans. A nestling tame or imprinted to humans (sees humans as its parents) can get into trouble after it fledges because it may beg food from humans and even attack them. So two basic principles should be adhered to:

1.   give the nestling as much association with its own species as possible, for example, by caging a nestling Brown Falcon with other injured adult or nestling Brown Falcons;

2.   never let the nestling associate humans with food.

Young hand-raised raptors should be fed with a simple cardboard puppet head, resembling the adult raptor's head. This cutout is folded over the tweezers that place meat into the nestling's mouth. Also, while feeding the chick, you can cover yourself (head included) with a formless sheet to avoid being seen by the nestling or you can feed it from behind a partition.

Overhandling

A common mistake made with young or injured raptors is overhandling. You should leave the chick inside a cardboard box lined with paper towels, handle it only when absolutely necessary, and then only with clean hands.

Sunlight

Some raptors, especially hawks and eagles, that are raised by humans will often develop rickets (splayed legs). They remain permanently crippled. Provided that the diet is correct, this illness usually is caused by a lack of adequate sunlight. Growing raptors, with the possible exception of falcons, shouldn't receive sunlight through glass, because glass filters out ultra-violet rays which are necessary for Vitamin D3 production. The chick in a cardboard box can be placed outside in direct sunlight for ten minutes a day, but you need to guard against very hot or very cold temperatures. Mid morning seems to be the best time of day. The nestling must always be safe from predators such as cats, and Australian Magpies which can kill the chick or carry it off in the briefest of unguarded moments.

Feeding

A nestling's first meal should be bite-sized pieces of meat that are small, soft and easily digested. You can use curved forceps or tweezers and a puppet (see above) to place food into the chick's open beak. For small chicks, 'Chupping' softly, in imitation of the parent's call, will usually elicit a begging response from them. The chick will reach upwards with its beak open.

Small quantities of fur and feathers can be included in the diet for raptors two weeks and older. When the nestling is old enough to stand strongly, you can leave whole carcasses of young fresh rats, quail or mice, split open to expose flesh. Check every few hours, preferably without the chick seeing you, to see if the chick is eating.

Fostering

The best possible way to release nestling raptors is to place them in the nest of the same species with similarly aged young. Many owls leave the nest before they can fly and, if found on the ground, people assume they are orphaned. Where possible it's best to find the nest they came from in the first place. Adult raptors won't reject nestlings handled by humans, but they may reject sick or weak nestlings and those that won't feed. Nestling raptors should be placed in a foster nest before they grow too big or become used to humans. If they are too old, they could leap from the nest as the climber leaves.

Examining Injured Raptors

Injured or orphaned raptors need to be examined. A complete examination should be carried out by a veterinarian but you can carry out a simple preliminary examination by starting from the head and working towards the tail (Figures 2 and 3). First determine the species from a field guide, then whether it is an adult or fledgling. Consider an "adult" raptor to be one with hunting experience and a fledgling to be nearly full grown but without hunting experience. In Australia most adults moult between October to April so you can examine the tail feathers, where they emerge from the body. If all these feathers are still growing, the bird is a fledgling but if none or only a few are growing it's an adult. Raptors, unlike chickens, are fully grown when they are fully feathered and this usually happens soon after they leave the nest.

The bird's head should be covered so you are less likely to be bitten and the wings, legs and feet can be stretched out for examination. A hood can be used if available.

Head: examine for injury or swelling.

Eyes: examine for injury, quite common in raptors; shine a torch into the raptor's eye in a darkened room to see if the pupil dilates. If it doesn't, neurological damage is indicated; if eyelids are closing the raptor may have a disease or its condition may be low.

Cere and Nostrils: note injury to the cere or blockage or discharge from nostrils; blood may indicate cranial trauma.

Beak: examine for fractures or splits as these commonly result from collision; check inside the mouth for lesions (cheesy whitish growths may be caused by *Trichomoniasis* blockage) or blood indicating an internal injury; listen for lung function, breathing should be quiet with no fluid or panting.

Neck: check for injury and for food in the crop.

Body: a sharp keel (*sternum*) indicates poor body condition; the preen gland at the base of the tail should appear normal and the feathers around it should be slightly oily; blood around the vent may indicate some internal injury; matting (excreta) around the vent could be worms, poor health or some internal injury.

Wings and legs: check for breaks or injury to bones or joints, count the 10 primaries on each wing; to check symmetry of its wings and legs, hold the body horizontal, with the wings free, and rock the bird gently from side to side; check for bumblefoot lesions, or other foot injuries, particularly on pads of the feet; check for feather loss.

Tail: count the 12 tail feathers and check for breakage and 'hunger traces' - marks across feathers causing weak points that are generally produced by stress, starvation, or if the feather is bent while still growing.

It is crucial that you keep the raptor calm and cool during this examination. If it is already sick or traumatised, overheating and/or stress will kill it. Because dehydration is an extremely common cause of death in sick, injured or young raptors, it is crucial to leave a dish of water with the raptor.

Injuries

Broken Bones and Wounds: Broken bones should be pinned by a veterinarian. Some breaks like those of the pelvis, cause temporary paralysis and will heal themselves if the bird is kept quiet for about 3 weeks. Open wounds are best kept clean, dry and uncovered. An injured raptor is best left alone with minimal handling, in a clean aviary. The wound should be thoroughly cleaned with Betadine solution and sprayed with Chloropel every two days. Some severe cuts or lacerations can be held closed with superglue. A sprained wing can be supported by a 'Figure 8' bandage (Figure 4) if you take care not to wrap it too tightly around the chest.

Feathers: Broken feathers can be repaired by 'imping'. This involves cutting the broken feather off cleanly and gluing in the same feather from another bird. This process is discussed in detail in *North American Falconry and Hunting Hawks* 1964 by Frank Beebe and Hal Webster, World Press, Denver, Colorado.

Housing

Raptors need access to wind, rain, shelter, sun and fresh air but they should also have shelter from the elements and protection from predators, like cats, dogs, foxes, and other raptors. The raptor's housing should reduce stress from humans and other fear-inducing elements.

With this in mind I describe below some ideas for flight pens that are suited to Australian conditions. Figures 5 and 6 show Robert Bartos' plan for converting a garage to housing for raptors. These designs are fairly open to the weather because raptors in Australia, or New Zealand, the southern United States or Mediterranean countries, are far more likely to die of heat stress than cold (hypothermia). They do need cover, to give them the option of avoiding rain, hail or snow storms. But direct rain appears to keep their plumage healthy and help their beak naturally flake so it's less likely to overgrow.

General Structure

Most raptors can't be kept in wire cages because they damage themselves, so vertical (not horizontal) dowels or slats are used. A room 3 metres high 3 metres wide and 6 metres long is adequate for most small and medium-sized raptors. Walls can be made of solid fibro or wood. The roof can be covered by 25 millimetre x 50 millimetre wooden slats with a 1 metre x 3 metre piece of corrugated iron across one end for shelter. Provide a window, either at floor level or at roof level, of vertical slats measuring 5 metres x 3 metres in the wall across one end of the structure.

Birds subject to disturbance should have the window at floor level (Figures 5 & 6). Consider the prevailing weather before building an enclosure. Our wet, stormy weather comes mainly from the south-west so we place structures on the north-east side of a hill and face windows north-east. Thus, the raptors are protected from the afternoon sun and inclement weather, but have access to direct morning sun. Wire cages can be made more suitable by stapling hessian over the wire on the inside of the cage.

Doors

Raptors can fly straight out of an open door so a safety curtain of canvas or a separate passageway outside the door is essential.

Obstructions

Nails, loose pieces of string or any objects that could entangle or damage raptors must be removed.

144

Floor

The floor should be of clean sand or pea (1 cm) sized gravel. Some smaller enclosures can have handles attached to the sides so they can be picked up or moved periodically to an area of clean ground.

Trees

For many species, particularly accipiters or Brown Falcons, you can build the cage around an existing tree, or plant one inside the cage. Wattle, *Acacia* species, grow quickly in the moist conditions inside the cage.

Glass

Raptors should never be housed behind glass. When they try to escape they fly into the glass and can die or be permanently paralysed.

Perches

The general principle in constructing perches is that captive birds are perched for more time and have less choice in perches than they have in the wild. Captive raptors have poorer circulation in their feet than wild raptors because they're less active and more prone to foot trouble like bumblefoot, a crippling infection in the pads of their feet. Bumblefoot can be prevented if you:

a)   Provide a variety of perches. Include several that are wider than the talon span of the raptor. Use perches suspended from the ceiling that move slightly while birds are perched on them.

b)   Use tires, coconut-fibre doormats and non-loop artificial doormats, and grass turf for perches. Coconut-fibre mats are quite comfortable to raptors and can be placed at an angle so perching raptors don't soil them.

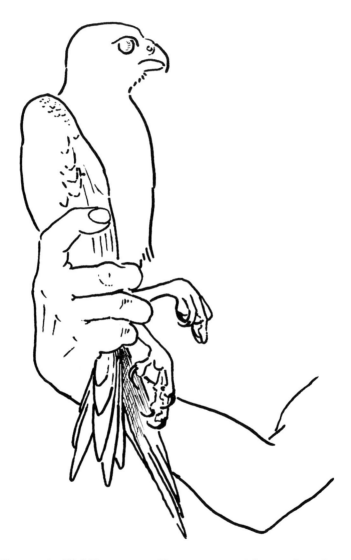

**Figure 1: Holding a smaller raptor with one hand.
It is important to separate the raptor's
legs with your fingers so its feet don't
grab each other or the tail.**

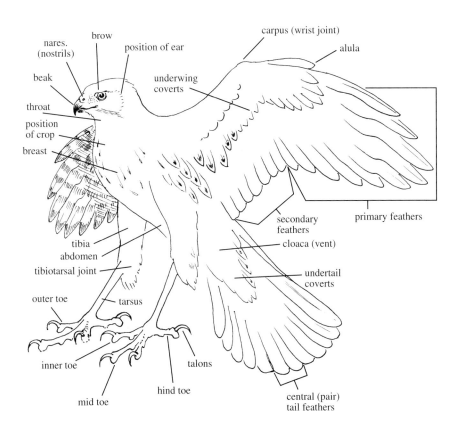

Figure 2: Body parts of a raptor

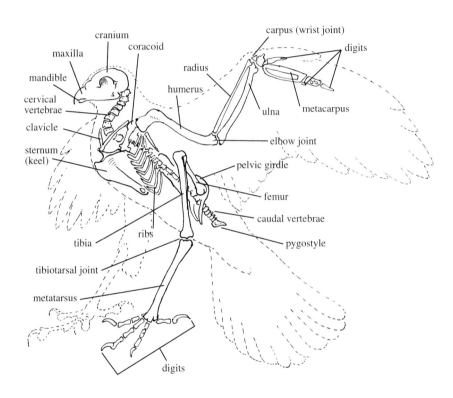

Figure 3: Skeleton of a raptor

Figure 4: Figure 8 bandage for sprain or broken radius or ulna

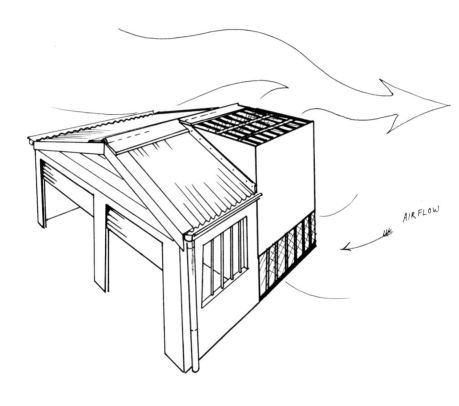

AIR FLOW

**Figure 5: Bartos design for converting a garage
to a raptor aviary**

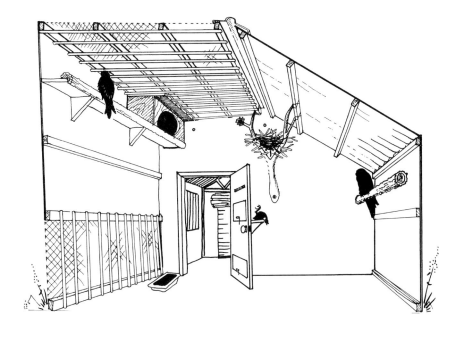

Figure 6: Structure inside a Bartos raptor aviary

Bath/Drinking Pans

Bath pans need to be long enough so that the raptor fits in, head to tail, but only deep enough to come up to the top of its legs. Plastic, wood or galvanised iron pigeon dishes work well. Bath pans 15 centimetres deep and 60 centimetres across are adequate for many small to medium raptors. Keep these filled with clean water.

Fire

Keep large bags and cardboard boxes available in case raptors need to be evacuated during a bush or aviary fire.

Diet

The general principles when acquiring food for raptors are to make it fresh, provide variety, and ensure that it is as similar as possible to food eaten in the wild. Raptors need to process bones, fur, feathers and insect casings to produce castings (pellets). So, where possible, use whole animals of an appropriate size for the raptor, that is, bird-eaters need appropriate-sized birds and mammal-eaters need appropriate-sized mammals. A good rule is to feed enough so there's a little left each day. Feed them once a day (three times a day for small nestlings), and keep in mind that birds require more food in cold weather. Food animals shouldn't be drugged or chemically killed.

> **Coturnix Quail** (*Coturnix coturnix*) - These are probably the best food available for bird-eating falcons and accipiters. They have small bones and feathers which raptors ingest, and females contain nutritious egg yolks.

> **Chickens** - Day-old cockerels are available from many hatcheries. They also contain egg yolk and help captive raptors attain the yellow colouring on the cere, legs and eye-ring that many have in the wild. However, day-old chicks are too low in calcium to be a complete food. Some raptors fed exclusively

on them die, and growing raptors can develop deficiencies. Five- to ten-week old chickens are more suitable.

Laboratory rats and mice - Acquired from universities, laboratories or medical schools, rats and mice are a suitable whole animal food for many raptors.

Road-Kills - In most places you can feed fresh road-killed birds and other animals in winter. Rabbits suffering from myxomatosis can safely be fed to raptors. But don't use road-kills in hot weather, or from agricultural areas where pesticides are used.

Beef - Fresh beef is suitable for a few weeks. The addition of a pinch of natural bone meal or DCP (*dicalcium phosphate*) makes beef a more balanced diet, but if beef or these additives are overused they can kill a raptor.

Pigeons, Sparrows and Starlings - Pigeons are highly nutritious but some carry poison and disease. They are poisoned in some cities and should never be fed to a raptor when fresh. Raptors can catch Trichomoniasis (frounce) and die if they aren't medicated in the early stages of the disease. Freezing seems to kill the protozoan *Trichomonas gallinae* that causes the disease. House Sparrows *Passer domesticus* and Starlings *Sturnus vulgaris* are excellent food, and the natural food of many bird-eaters like Australian Hobbies and Peregrines. Again, you have to take care with poisons and pesticides that could be passed on to the raptor.

Foods vary in nutritional value and the white meat of rabbits or chickens will not sustain a small raptor like an Australian Hobby. They need additional red meats like sparrows, beef or pigeons. Many older works argue that raptors should have lean, not fatty, meat. However, birds low in condition need as much

fat as possible to increase their weight so offer them
as much as they will eat.

Transporting Raptors

The general principles for transporting raptors are (a) keep
the bird cool and calm and; (b) prevent feather and cere
damage.

(i)   The best container for transport is a darkened cardboard box or airline 'pet pack' with
a hessian or towelling floor the raptor can
grip. The container must be large enough
for the bird to turn around without damag-
ing its tail or wings. The best way to mini-
mise stress and keep the bird quiet is to
darken the box but allow ample circulation.

(ii)   Raptors shouldn't be transported on hot
days (over 30^0C) or in hot airless vehicles.
Airliners are generally cool but raptors can
overheat while waiting to be placed on the
aircraft. If raptors are fully grown and
healthy, low temperatures are no problem
to them.

(iii)   Provision of food or water for adults is un-
necessary for trips of 24 hours or less.

(iv)   When it is removed from the container, a
raptor's talons should be carefully dislodged
from the hessian or towelling because talons and toes of nestling raptors can be damaged. To prevent its escape, the raptor
should be removed from the box inside a
room or the destination aviary.

Determining when raptors are ready for release

The important cosiderations for release are:

1. health of the bird
2. its relationship with humans, and
3. locality and time of release

These three criteria appear straightforward but, to judge them successfully, require considerable experience and assessment:

1.   Health of the bird

(a)   General - The first consideration should be general condition. The raptor should have recovered completely and have no broken feathers. The feathers should have a sheen on them and be waterproof. Talons and beak should be near perfect and the bird should be in good condition. That is, the muscle on either side of the sternum should be convex. This is best achieved by unlimited feeding while the raptor is housed in a large, undisturbed aviary.

(b)   Flying ability - This can be difficult to ascertain. If you fly the raptor using falconry techniques, its flying ability can be assessed subjectively or with the aid of video cameras. For small raptors, such as Kestrels, flying in a large aviary gives a reasonable indication of their flying ability.

Another test of a raptor's flying ability requires at least two people and a piece of strong nylon line. The bird is attached to the line by jesses and a swivel. One person releases the bird and the other lightly grips the line with gloves. This provides a gentle brake that slows the bird to a stop after about 30 metres. This technique can be dangerous - the bird can come suddenly to the end of the line and break its leg. Never tie the end of the line to a solid object. Instead, tie a light block of wood to the end of the line that drags the flying raptor and slows it down if the line has slipped from the gloved hands. After the handler has experience with several releases, this technique gives a reasonable indication of flying ability, particularly if you fly the raptor twice upwind and twice downwind, to carefully judge strength and symmetry of its wingbeats. Falcons, such as Brown Falcons or kestrels, that catch slow, ground-oriented prey can be released with slightly asymmetrical flight, that is, they may fly with one wing very slightly lower than the other. Other species, such as Peregrines and Australian Hobbies, can't be released with a slightly damaged wing because they won't be able to catch their main prey, fast-flying birds.

2. **Locality and time of release**

    Time

    Ornithologists can help with release times and localities. Seasonal considerations are important. Winter on the Northern and Southern Tablelands of New South Wales is bleak and raptors such as Australian Kestrels tend to move to lower altitudes and warmer latitudes. Conversely, in central Australia winter can be the best time of year for food, but summers are harsh and raptors such as Black Falcons may move out. Because inclement weather can prevent some raptors from hunting, consult a weather forecast before the release.

    Locality

    Raptors should be released:

    (1) into their natural habitat, for example, open inland areas for Black Falcons. Where possible, release them in the area where they originally came from.

(2) where their natural food is abundant. Accessibility of food is important because high grass or heavy bush can make prey unavailable to some raptors.

(3) away from territories of conspecifics or incompatible species, for example, Little Eagles and Wedge-tailed Eagles. Australian Magpies and many raptors can mob just-released raptors and this is highly stressful to the newly released bird. Choose release sites with few of these birds.

'Staging areas' can be used, that is, localities where you release most of your raptors and they remain for a time, while you feed them until they move on. A good 'staging area' usually has abundant, available prey to keep the raptor present but is a poor area for breeding because of disturbance from humans or a lack of nest sites. Areas near a city or farm can be great 'staging areas' and locals can help monitor the released bird.

Hack

A nestling hand-raised raptor that has no hunting experience will probably starve if you release it. Raptors don't need their parents to teach them to hunt but they do need practice in learning to hunt. Hack is a technique that gives a raptor this hunting experience and helps them develop independence and strength, so they aren't dependent on humans for food. This ancient method was described in detail by Frederick II of Hoehenstaufen circa 1250 A.D. and was probably used long before then. Hack involves the use of a hack-room or hack-box as an intermediate stage in the release process.

A hack box can be .5 metre x .5 metre x .5 metre with a large hole .25 metre x .25 metre in the front covered with bars so raptors can see out but can't get out. The box is placed up in a tree or on a building away from cats so the raptors have a commanding view of surrounding paddocks and can 'imprint' on this terrain. They are fed every day on a ledge or board at the entrance hole so, when the bars are lifted and they are free, they know to come back to this ledge for food.

Nestlings are placed in the box about two weeks before they can fly, when they're about two-thirds feathers and one-third down. When fully feathered and ready to fly (about 8 weeks with eagles, 6 weeks with Peregrines, Black and Brown Falcons and about 5 weeks with Kestrels, Hobbies and goshawks) the bars in front of the hole are lifted at night when the nestlings can't see. Two days supply of frozen food is tied to the food ledge and the hack box is not visited by humans for two days. Raptors at hack are like wild raptors and if they see humans just before their initial flight they will fledge prematurely, and fly just strongly enough so that humans can't catch them. These hacked nestlings will have no adults to guide them back to the box and will probably starve.

The nestlings can be monitored from a distance with binoculars. It's fun to watch them walk out on the food ledge, then onto branches and finally, to see them take their first flight. After two days, start to tie food daily to the hack board so they can't carry it down into the long grass and eat without being seen. This way you can see if the raptors are still around. After that, it's a matter of enjoying the raptors' daily flight and hunting practice, their play and adventures, until they drift off in two to six weeks.

Sometimes inexperienced Brown Falcons, Wedge-tailed Eagles, Brown Goshawks and other mammal-eating raptors can learn to hunt if released into areas with very high rabbit populations, particularly if myxomatosis has been introduced into the rabbits. Young Kestrels, Collared Sparrowhawks, Brown Goshawks, Brown Falcons and some other species hunt insects soon after they fledge in the wild so captive birds that haven't hunted can sometimes be released into areas with high concentrations of mice or insects. This release method will not work with bird-catching falcons.

Rehabilitating injured and orphaned raptors back to the wild is rewarding. Many carers view it as 'redressing the balance' because most of these birds were injured or orphaned by human actions in the first place. Rehabilitation also puts us close to a wild creature for a time. We can nurture it until release day then feel, vicariously, the sensation of freedom and independence that wild raptors, by right, should know.

*   In Victoria, the National Parks and Wildlife Division of the Department of Conservation, Forests and Lands; in Tasmania, the Department of Lands, Parks and Wildlife; in the ACT the ACT Parks and Wildlife Service; in the Northern Territory the NT Conservation Commission and in other states, the National Parks and Wildlife Service.

Jerry Olsen was born in Salt Lake City in 1948 and grew up in Spokane Washington before moving to Australia in 1972. He has a son and a daughter, lives in Canberra and lectures in the Applied Ecology Research Group and the Faculty of Education at the University of Canberra.

Jerry has studied birds of prey since boyhood and his other books include *Caring For Birds of Prey* 1990 and *Birds of Prey and Game Birds of Australia* (with P. Olsen and F. Crome) 1993.